The

BIBLE

In Story
And Pictures

The
BIBLE
In Story and Pictures

REVISED FROM THE ORIGINAL EDITION
OF "THE CHILDREN'S STORY BIBLE" BY

Harold Begbie
Author of "Twice Born Men"

ILLUSTRATED BY
Cyrus LeRoy Baldridge
Herbert Morton Stoops
Elliott Means
and Steele Savage

H. S. STUTTMAN CO., *Publishers*
New York 16, N. Y.

Introduction

THE NEW PICTORIAL EDITION of The Children's Story Bible by Harold Begbie is intended to help people understand the timeless truths of the Word of God. The Bible is more than ancient history. It has a message for our own day. Through it God speaks the great words which have endured through the centuries and form the only secure foundation for life in any generation.

The Bible is essentially the one story of God's outreaching love and His longing to enter into the life of mankind. It describes His efforts to develop a universal family of those who will live together as His children and as brothers of each other. The chief character in the Bible is always God. Open it at random and immediately you will be reminded of Him. But since He works through people, the Scriptures are filled with stories about men and women, good and bad, who have accepted or rejected His purposes of love and righteousness. Until one is familiar with these stories he is not fully equipped for life, for they embody the great ideas which God is seeking to instill into the minds of all those whom He has created.

Stories such as those which Begbie has selected from the Old Testament illustrate the moral and spiritual principles which need to be learned anew in every age. The creation of the world and the origin of life as an act of God, Adam's and Eve's unhappiness because of their refusal to obey God, Job's patience in affliction and sorrow, the forgiving love of Joseph for the brothers who tried to kill him and his concern for his aged father, Moses' burning indignation against injustice, the danger of undedicated strength like that of Samson, the loyalty of Ruth and Esther, David's penitence for his sin, Jonah's inability to run away from God, the courage of the prophets in declaring unwelcome truth—such stories strengthen and enrich the lives of those who read them. No one can question their value.

The Old Testament finds its fulfillment in the New Testament. The Bible comes to its climax in "the greatest story ever told about the greatest Man who ever lived." The revelation of God's love in Jesus Christ has been the mightiest power in history. Some unknown writer has well said that "all the armies that ever marched, all the navies ever built, all the kings that ever reigned, and all the parliaments that ever sat, put together, have not influenced this planet as has that One Solitary Life."

The basic facts in the life of Christ are told by Begbie in simple sincerity. Many of the great passages from the gospels are quoted directly from the King James version of the Bible. Following the record of Christ's life on earth comes the story of His living Spirit and His influence in the lives of the early Christians. Delightful character sketches are given of the twelve Apostles. The pages describing the work of Paul and the spread of Christianity throughout the ancient world are vividly written and constitute a masterpiece. They create a deeper appreciation of the Apostle's greatness. All these stories are universal in their appeal. They contain the great truths by which men must always live and should become a part of the common education of children and youth.

Because of its acknowledged importance to mankind, the Bible has long been the world's best seller. It has been translated into more than a thousand different languages and dialects. But at the same time there is a serious question about the extent to which it is read. Most young people, even though they have been enrolled for years in a Sunday School, seem lamentably ignorant of its contents. Gallup polls have shown that many people cannot even tell the difference between the Old Testament and the New. There is a danger that the Bible has become the book which everyone owns but seldom reads. A chaplain in the American army during the second World War was so disturbed by the Biblical illiteracy of the soldiers that he declared, "Bruce Barton was right when he called the Bible 'The Book Nobody Knows.' "

The chief reason the Bible is not better known is because it is difficult to understand. People are confused by the fact that it is not simply one book but a library of 66 different books, most of which were written at different times by different authors. It tells about people who lived thousands of years ago in an Oriental country. Their manners and customs are in marked contrast to our own. Most people have never had the privilege of travel in Palestine and have no knowledge of its geography or appearance.

If the Bible is to be interesting to the average reader, and especially to children, it must be put in words easily understood, and illustrated by pictures that make vivid its meaning. Many authors have produced books based on the Bible but no one tells the message of the Scriptures in story form better than Harold Begbie. With the skill of a trained reporter, he selects the essential elements and does not get lost in unnecessary detail. His reverent approach, his beauty of style, and his careful choice of materials have combined to produce a book which is completely true to the Bible itself. It will lead young and old to turn to the sacred Book with new appreciation and enjoyment.

The pictures in this book constitute an attractive feature. It is significant that Jesus never lost an opportunity to get people to use their eyes. Continually He reenforced his teaching by pointing to the objects that were around Him. "Look at the flowers," He said. "See the birds." "Behold the sower." He called attention to the trees, the sunset, and the clouds. No one can doubt that the vividness of Jesus' teaching is one reason for its lasting hold on the minds of men. Anyone with experience in trying to transmit ideas knows that they are more effectively communicated when pictures are used to supplement the verbal message. The full color art reproductions, photographs and drawings in this book show the settings, and backgrounds of Biblical events and make it easier to understand the words which God is speaking through the Bible. Boys and girls gladly listen to a story but remember it longer when it is accompanied by pictures which help to create a greater sense of reality.

No generation of people needs the Bible more than our own. The world stands at the crossroads of an atomic age. Men must learn to live together or they will at last destroy themselves. And they must have adequate spiritual resources if they are to face successfully the tensions and temptations of modern life. Everyone needs to build his life in such a way that the pressure from the outside world is balanced by sustaining strength within the individual soul.

More attention needs to be paid to helping members of the younger generation develop spiritual resources. "The most beautiful sight in all the world," said Confucius, "is a child walking confidently down the road after you have shown him the way." It is not easy in our day, however, to give children the directions that will enable them to walk down the highway of the future with courage and faith. They need a map which helps to mark out their course, and also a continuing source of inner strength. No other book meets such needs so well as does the Bible. It is the most dependable moral and religious guide known to mankind.

If THE BIBLE IN STORY AND PICTURES helps people to understand the Bible more clearly and follow it more closely, it will have fulfilled the purpose of its publishers.

The

BIBLE

In Story

And Pictures

———— ❖ ————

THE OLD TESTAMENT

CONTENTS

Stories and Pictures from The Old Testament

*And the waters under Heaven He gathered
into one place and called them the Seas.
And the dry land appeared, shining and glad,
out of the midst of the seas, and God called
the dry land Earth.*

The Bible Story of Creation

IN THE BEGINNING, before God created the earth, there was only a great darkness. There was nothing which had any shape or form. There were no stars, no warm, bright sun, no wind blowing. There was no earth, no sky, no heat and cold—just darkness, silence, and water everywhere.

But God was there. His Spirit moved upon the face of the waters; and God said, "Let there be light." And there was light.

So God did two things. He broke the awful silence, and He created Light. He divided the light from the darkness. And He called

"And God said, 'Let the earth bring forth grass, the herb yielding seed, and the fruit tree yielding fruit after his kind, whose seed is in itself, upon the earth': and it was so." (Gen. 1:11)

the light Day, and He called the darkness Night. Then God divided the waters, setting Heaven in the midst of them. And the waters under Heaven He gathered into one place and called them the Seas. And the dry land appeared, shining and glad, out of the midst of the seas, and God called the dry land Earth.

Then out of the dry land, grass came forth, and many strange and lovely herbs, and trees throwing their shadow on the grass. God made the herb and the fruit tree, each with its own seed, so that they could sow themselves and gradually cover the earth with beauty and cooling shade.

And God filled the sky above the earth with stars. He gave the sun power to rule the day and the moon power to rule the night.

And then, there came a greater wonder still. Out of the deep waters upon the earth God called forth Life. He spoke, and from the water issued living things that could move and utter sound, and swim and fly—tiny and unseen things, millions of them; huge and mighty things, thousands of them. And the earth brought forth living things. So that the earth, the water, the land and the air became filled with life.

And after that, God said: "Let us make man in our image, after our likeness; and let them have dominion over the fish of the sea, and over the fowl of the air, and over the cattle, and over all the earth, and over every creeping thing that creepeth upon the earth."

The Garden of Eden

"And the Lord God formed man of the dust of the ground, and breathed into his nostrils the breath of life; and man became a living soul.

"And the Lord God planted a garden eastward in Eden; and there he put the man whom he had formed." The name of this man was Adam.

"And out of the ground the Lord God formed every beast of the

18

They had to leave the garden of Eden

field, and every fowl of the air; and brought them unto Adam to see what he would call them:

"And Adam gave names to all cattle, and to the fowl of the air, and to every beast of the field"; but he had no human companion like himself. So God gave him yet one more great gift. He caused a deep sleep to come upon Adam, and while he slept the Lord took one of his ribs, and out of it He made a woman. And Adam called her name Eve.

These two then, Adam and Eve his wife, lived together in the beautiful garden God had made for them, and for a time they were happy and content. The animals came to them when they were called; the birds sang over their heads as they walked; and the fishes came to the side of the lake to watch them as they stood in the sunlight.

God had given them everything on the earth, with one exception. They were not to eat of the fruit growing on a certain tree in the garden. There were a thousand other fruits of which they might eat, but this one was forbidden. It was God's test of their love for Him.

But one day the wicked Tempter, the Evil One, took the form of a serpent and glided into the garden. He sought out Eve when she was not with Adam, and suggested to her that she should eat of the forbidden fruit; that it would make her wise, and would not harm her.

Eve did not obey the Evil One, but she did not drive him away. She stayed and argued with him. And when the serpent had gone, the temptation to eat the fruit stayed in her mind; she allowed herself to think about it. At last the temptation was too great for her. She ate the fruit, and took it to Adam, her husband, and persuaded him also to do this forbidden thing.

Then Adam and Eve heard the voice of the Lord God "walking in the garden in the cool of the day," and they were afraid and hid themselves in the trees. And God said that because they had done evil they must suffer. The punishment He sent them was not a cruel

A Palestine Arab with primitive plow, near the ancient wall of Jerusalem—turning the soil as did his ancestors thousands of years ago.

punishment, but He would not let them live any longer in their happy garden. Instead, He made them go out into the world to toil for their existence.

The Story of Cain and Abel

TWO sons were born to Adam and Eve. The first was named Cain; the second, Abel. Cain, when he grew up, became a gardener; Abel became a shepherd. Adam and Eve told their sons about God, Creator of the world, and the two brothers learned to worship Him.

But there was a difference between the characters of these two brothers. Cain, as he dug the soil and tended his plants, did not have a love of God in his heart and sin crept into his life. Abel, as he wandered through the valley with his flocks, tried to please God in all that he did.

Now, the way these two men worshiped God was by sacrifice. That is to say, they gave up something which was theirs, and offered it to God, just as in our day people give up money for God. Cain gave some of his fruits and Abel gave some of his flocks.

But Cain's sacrifice was made grudgingly. It was a sulky gift. He gave because he was afraid not to give. Abel, with purer heart and nobler soul, gave of his very best to God, and gave cheerfully.

When Cain saw that Abel's sacrifice was better than his, instead of making his own equal to it, he hated Abel. He became jealous, or envious.

He would think bitterly of Abel as he dug in his garden or walked home through the fields at sunset. He would hate his

brother for being better than himself. So long did he dwell on this
angry thought that at last he could think of nothing else.

One day the two brothers met in the fields, and began to argue
some point. In the midst of the argument, rage suddenly seized
upon Cain. With a wild and desperate fury he sprang upon his
brother, struck him, and killed him.

In an instant Cain heard the voice of God saying to him:

"Where is Abel, thy brother?"

"I know not," he cried back. "Am I my brother's keeper?"

But the Voice in his soul continued:

"What hast thou done? The voice of thy brother's blood crieth
unto Me from the ground."

Cain knew then the horror of his crime. He had done something
which could not be undone. A moment before Abel had been a living man; now he lay dead and still. Cain could never restore him.

With a bitter cry of agony, he called upon God:

"My punishment is greater than I can bear."

Cain then knew the horror of his crime

Henceforth there could be no rest for him, no hours of peace and contentment; no days of happiness and joy. For God placed the mark of a murderer upon him. In his heart was despair.

"And Cain went out from the presence of the Lord, and dwelt in the land of Nod, on the east of Eden."

The Story of Noah's Ark

AS TIME passed, men and women finally became so wicked that God was sorry He had made them. He looked at the way in which people were living, and determined to punish them by sending a great flood. But God remembered that on earth there was one noble and saintly man, Noah. Noah was just and perfect, and for the sake of this upright man, God saved the earth from destruction.

He called Noah, and bade him build a great boat, called an ark, out of gopher wood, with rooms in it for his wife and his sons, and his sons' wives, and with one great window in it, and with a mighty door in the side. This great ark was to be covered with pitch inside and outside, and was to be built so well that it should have room for seven of every clean beast, and two of the others, with food for the animals and for Noah and his family.

Noah obeyed God. He built the ark, and when the warning came he called to the ark two of every living thing upon the earth—animals, birds and insects; and laying in a great quantity of food, he himself, and his wife and his children, with all these other living things, entered the ark.

One of the 400 ancient cedars of Lebanon, hundreds of years old. Noah's ark was probably built of cedar or cypress wood, called "gopher wood" in the Bible (Gen. 6:14), though not mentioned elsewhere.

Noah gives thanks to the Lord after the flood! (Gen. 8:20) *Noah's Sacrifice,* by Cavallino. (From the Kress Collection, National Gallery of Art.)

Forty days and nights of rain

Then the springs of the earth and the fountains of the sea burst their bounds, the windows of the heavens were opened, and the water covered the highest mountains. And in the flood the wicked perished.

But God remembered Noah. After forty days and nights the rain ceased, the waters ceased rising, and sunlight entered the ark. Then Noah let a raven fly loose from the window of the ark, and it did not come back to him. Later Noah sent out a dove, but the dove flew terrified above the waters, and returned to the window of the ark. After seven days more Noah sent the dove out again, and this time it returned bearing in its beak an olive leaf. Noah then knew that the earth was dry, and when he again sent the dove forth it did not return.

With great joy Noah came out from the ark with his family. They led the animals down from the ark on to the dry land, and set the birds free; and on an altar of stones they offered thanks to God. God was pleased with Noah, and set a bow of light in the sky after the rain. That was the first rainbow, and it is beautiful to think that God set it in the sky to tell the world that He would never again send a flood to destroy the earth.

The Tower of Babel

THE ark rested in a place where it was easy for the sons of Noah to spread themselves over the earth. This was the intention of God. He wanted men to cross into all lands and cultivate the whole earth. But the sons of Noah settled down in one place, and they built a great city, and in the midst of the city they erected a vast tower.

When God saw that they were determined to disobey Him, He visited the foolish city, and caused the people to speak in different languages, so that no one could understand the other.

So the Lord scattered them abroad from thence upon the face of all the earth: and they left off to build the city. Therefore is the name of it called Babel. because the Lord did there confound the language of all the earth: and from thence did the Lord scatter them abroad upon the face of all the earth.

But even after God had made a mock of this foolish Tower of Babel, men continued to do foolish things, contrary to His law. Instead of praying to God, they made idols, or statues, or images and called them gods, and prayed to them. This is called idolatry.

God wished man to understand that everything they saw with their eyes—the sun, fire, animals, the whole world—was the work of His hands. He wanted them to understand that the sun only warmed them and made the earth beautiful because He had ordained it. He wanted man to be, not a coward, but a strong, intelligent creature, trusting in the power of the great Creator, and setting himself to get dominion over the earth.

They made images and prayed to them

Nimrod, the Mighty Hunter

AT THIS time there lived in the world a man by the name of Nimrod, who was a mighty hunter before the Lord. He was so strong that other people could not stand up against him. They came under his power and he ruled over them. He gathered people about him and went across the earth conquering cities, and set up a kingdom in which he was the ruler.

But Nimrod's empire was poisoned by idolatry; for although it included mighty cities, the people who dwelt in them were weak and sinful. They made images and prayed to them. They were superstitious and worshiped certain animals.

God could not be pleased with such people. He had ordained that men should have dominion over the earth. How could men become great who trembled at a shadow, groveled in the dust before images, and even worshiped animals?

It is said that Job once sat under this flourishing oak tree on Druse Mountain in a plateau south of Damascus, Syria, known in the Bible as the Hauran (Ezekiel 47:16-18). Nearby are the stone ruins said to be the house in which Job lived.

The Patience of Job

YET all men at that time were not so sunk in folly and wickedness. There was one, at least, who had the soul of a hero. This was that great and splendid spirit, Job.

Job was a rich man. He was a great lord, the master of servants, the owner of much land, the farmer of many flocks and herds. In addition, he was a happy man, living cheerfully in the midst of his family, enjoying life with a good appetite, and praising God, Who had blessed him with so much happiness and comfort.

There were, no doubt, many who said: "It is easy for this great lord to believe in God, but how would it be with him if he became poor and miserable like us? Where would his faith be then? It is easy enough to be good when you are rich."

But God tried Job. A storm arose from the desert, and swept down upon a house in which Job's children were assembled, crushing them to death. Another storm destroyed his flocks; robbers made away with his camels, his oxen, and his asses; and upon himself there fell the terrible and awful doom of leprosy. His wife fled from him; his friends abandoned him; the stricken man was left alone, childless, deserted and cursed, smitten with sores from the soles of his feet to the crown of his head. In this appalling ruin Job uttered words which we say to this day when we bury our dead: "The Lord gave, and the Lord hath taken away; blessed be the Name of the Lord."

But Job was not perfect, and when three of his old friends journeyed to see him from far countries, and comforted him by saying he must have sinned to bring this calamity upon his head (such are

33

called Job's comforters), he suddenly rebelled against his doom, and cursed the day that he was born.

In the argument which followed between Job and his comforters, the poor, smitten man regained some of his faith, and uttered many noble words concerning the wisdom of God. But finally God showed Job the whole truth of the matter. He showed that no man can judge God: first, because no man existed when God created the heavens and the earth, and therefore does not know His purposes; and, secondly, because no living man has passed through the gates of Death, and therefore none can know what God has prepared for us in the endless ages of eternity.

These are some of the mighty words, unequaled in all the books of the world, which came to Job from God:

Who is this that darkeneth counsel by words without knowledge?

Who wast thou when I laid the foundations of the earth? . . . when the morning stars sang together, and all the sons of God shouted for joy?

Have the gates of death been opened unto thee? Or hast thou seen the doors of the shadow of death?

Canst thou bind the sweet influences of Pleiades, or loose the bands of Orion?

Knowest thou the ordinances of heaven? Canst thou set the dominion thereof in the earth?

Hast thou given the horse strength? Hast thou clothed his neck with thunder?

Doth the hawk fly by thy wisdom? Doth the eagle mount up at thy command?

Shall he that contendeth with the Almighty instruct him? He that reproveth God, let him answer it!

Then Job answered, and said:

Behold, I am vile: what shall I answer Thee? I will lay mine hand upon my mouth.

This gnarled tree seems to signify the struggle for existence which characterizes man's short life. "For there is hope of a tree, if it be cut down, that it will sprout again . . ." (Job 14:7)

"Behold, I am vile"

So when God had tried Job, and had made him humble and obedient, He blessed him again, giving him even more good things than he had had in the beginning. Seven strong sons and three lovely daughters were born to Job, and he lived to see four generations of his children and grandchildren. So Job lived in happiness, honor and health, praising God all his days.

Abraham, the Friend of God

ACROSS the vast Syrian desert a procession of men and camels made its way, from the direction of Mesopotamia. Among the men was a tall and noble chieftain named Abraham, whose eyes often gazed across the terrible desert, as though in quest of some end to his journey. By his side went a younger man, his nephew, Lot.

It was a sad journey they were making, and only the iron will of Abraham kept the others to their duty. For the people of this cavalcade were moving away from their homes, from their friends, from people who spoke their own language and whose customs were the same as their own; and they were journeying to discover a new country, where everything would be strange to them, and where, perhaps, they might encounter enemies and treachery, and meet with slavery and death.

We can understand how Abraham's wife, the beautiful Sarah, listened to the complaints of her women, and sometimes shared their terrors, and sometimes even questioned the wisdom of her husband. When, at each day's end, the tents were erected and the camels knelt down to rest in the sand, when darkness fell across the great round circle of the desert, and under the shining stars men and women sat silently about the fires thinking of the comfortable homes they had left behind, even the young Lot may have felt rebellious toward his uncle.

But no one dared to withstand this splendid king of men, Abraham. He heard God speak to him and he obeyed the word of God. How the men and women must have looked across the dark of the

A caravan of camels, the "ships
of the desert," winds along the
Palestine coast at sunset.

A Holy Land farmer tends his cattle in
"the plain of Jordan . . . well watered
everywhere . . ." (Gen. 13:10)

The valley of the River Jordan, as it
might have appeared to Abraham and
his nephew, Lot. (Gen. 13:5-12)

The plain of Esraelon, with Nazareth in the distance. The Israelites fought many battles with fierce enemies on this broad, fertile plain.

Journeying to discover a new country

encampment towards this grand old man, with the firelight on his rugged face and snowy beard, this old man, who declared that the God of Heaven had spoken to him—this old man who made his journey across the desert to find the Land that had been promised to him.

These were the words Abraham declared God had addressed to him:

Get thee out of thy country, and from thy kindred, and from thy father's house, unto a land that I will shew thee. And I will make of thee a great nation, and I will bless thee, and make thy name great and thou shalt be a blessing. And I will bless them that bless thee, and curse him that curseth thee and in thee shall all families of the earth be blessed.

It was this command, this magnificent promise, which kept Abraham upon his way. The end of the long journey came at last, and Abraham found himself in Palestine, a lovely and a fertile country, beautiful to the eye and comfortable to the heart. Glad and grateful were the hearts of his company as they gazed upon this gracious land.

Here Abraham dwelt, he and all his people; and they grew very

rich, and fortune smiled upon them. But so rich and powerful did they become that jealousy crept in between the shepherds and herdmen of Abraham and the shepherds and herdmen of Lot, his nephew.

How Abraham Parted from Lot and Befriended Him

Then Abraham said to his nephew:

Let there be no strife, I pray thee, between me and thee, and between my herdmen and thy herdmen, for we are brethren. Is not the whole land before thee? Separate thyself, I pray thee, from me. If thou wilt take the left hand, then I will go to the right; or if thou depart to the right hand, then I will go to the left.

43

These gracious words were spoken on a high tableland; and Lot, turning from his uncle, looked down to the beautiful valley south of the Jordan, stretching far away in richness and loveliness, and promising great happiness and wealth. This was his choice, and Abraham parted from his·nephew with love and kindness.

Afterward, when he heard that his nephew had been involved in a great war, and had been carried away a prisoner, Abraham did not forget him, but armed his servants and went in pursuit of the captors, and prevailed against them. After the victory Abraham refused any reward for his help, saying that he would take nothing, "from a thread even to a shoelatchet."

He returned to his pastoral life, and again God visited him in visions, with the assurance that his children should inherit the earth.

Abraham's Wife and
Hagar, the Little Egyptian Maid

In the midst of this peaceful and pleasant existence, Sarah, the wife of Abraham, had many sad and tragic thoughts. She was, as we shall see, a strange mixture of strength and weakness, kindness and unkindness. We know that she was exceedingly beautiful, for a king of Egypt had greatly desired her for his wife, and we know that Abraham was devotedly in love with her. She must have thought many times of God's promise that Abraham's children should inherit the earth; and as the days went by, and no son came, she began at last to fear that she was unworthy to be Abraham's wife.

In those days men married more than one wife, and Sarah went one day to Abraham, and persuaded him to take for a second wife a little Egyptian maid in her service, named Hagar.

She said to Abraham, "Marry my slave girl, and perhaps she will give us a son for our home." So Abraham did what his wife said. When Hagar found herself so honored, she was at first a little proud, and her pride made Sarah angry. Sarah drove her out with angry words, and the little slave girl, who had been so proud and conceited, found herself suddenly an outcast in the wilderness. While she was weeping there, God sent a messenger to tell her that she must return to Sarah. "Return to thy mistress, and submit thyself under her hands." And the poor, frightened slave girl exclaimed in words that ever since have been spoken in all languages in all countries, "Thou God seest me." She went back obediently and submitted herself to the harshness of Sarah. Hagar and Abraham had a son, Ishmael.

One day, as Abraham sat in the door of his tent, when the sun was at its highest and the land lay dazed in an Eastern noon, there suddenly appeared before him three strangers. Abraham rose, struck by their wondrous appearance, and received them with the highest honor. While he was entertaining these visitors, one of them foretold that Sarah should have a son.

We can imagine the joy of the old father and mother. When the child Isaac was born the preparations made by the rejoicing parents for the feast passed everything they had ever done in splendor and magnificence. Sarah was just as excited as Abraham, and she laughed often in her joy.

Ishmael, Hagar's son, the lad who hitherto had been everything to Abraham, looked on, and laughed mockingly, so that Sarah, in

There suddenly appeared three strangers

Beersheba, the town frequently referred to in the Bible as the southern limit of Palestine. Digging a well at Beersheba is attributed to Abraham (Gen. 22:19) and Isaac, and it was into the wilderness of Beersheba that Hagar wandered with Ishmael. (Gen. 21:14)

Peasant women of the Holy Land, their garments perhaps differing little from those worn by women in the days of Abraham. (Gen. 16:1-16)

an outburst of rage, called to Abraham, "Cast out this bondwoman and her son; for the son of this bondwoman shall not be heir with my son."

A Voice Comforts Abraham
for the Loss of His Son Ishmael

Abraham grieved because he loved his son Ishmael; but a Voice comforted him, saying, "Let it not be grievous in thy sight because of the lad, and because of thy bondwoman; in all that Sarah hath said unto thee, hearken unto her voice; for in Isaac shall thy seed be called. And also of the son of the bondwoman will I make a nation, because he is thy seed."

Abraham listened to this Voice in his soul, and he trusted it. He brought himself to the great agony of parting with his son, the gay and spirited young Ishmael. There is something very touching in the brief story of this parting. Abraham rose up "early in the morning," evidently before his angry wife was stirring, and, providing poor Hagar and his son with food and water, took a loving farewell of them, telling them, we may be sure, of God's promise, and watching them through tears in his eyes as they departed.

Alas! for poor Hagar. She set out very sorrowfully, making no protest, but quietly submitting to her hard fate. When her food and water came to an end, and they could go no farther, she laid her son down and went a long way off from him, saying, "Let me not see the death of the child." And she wept.

God's Promise to Hagar

And God heard the voice of the lad; and the angel of God called to Hagar out of Heaven, and said unto her, What aileth thee, Hagar? Fear not, for God hath heard the voice of the lad where he is.

Arise, lift up the lad, and hold him in thine hand; for I will make him a great nation.

This new road from Beersheba to Sodom, where Lot's wife "looked back from behind him, and she became a pillar of salt" (Gen. 19:26), winds through territory where Abraham, Isaac and Jacob settled, ending near copper mines dating from the days of King Solomon.

And God opened her eyes, and she saw a well of water; and she went and filled the bottle with water, and gave the lad drink.

And God was with the lad; and he grew, and dwelt in the wilderness, and became an archer.

And he dwelt in the wilderness of Paran; and his mother took him a wife out of the land of Egypt.

But another and a greater sacrifice lay before him. God tested his faith by telling him to take his son Isaac and offer him as a burnt offering on the mountains. What a frightful command! And how Abraham must have shrunk from it! We can imagine how he tried to persuade himself that it was not God who had spoken to him, that it was only a dream, a thing he should put out of his mind and forget. But Abraham's glory was this—he listened whenever God spoke, he trusted in God and went forward in obedience to His will.

The Terrible Trial That Came to Abraham

So he rose up early in the morning, and saddled an ass, and split wood for the fire, and took with him Isaac and two young men, and started out upon his journey of death. At the end of three days in the mountains he saw the place appointed by God for the sacrifice. And Abraham said unto his young men, "Abide ye here with the ass, and I and the lad will go yonder and worship, and come again to you." Then Isaac said suddenly, "My father! Behold the fire and the wood; but where is the lamb for a burnt offering?" And Abraham, in great trouble, answered, "My son, God will provide Himself a lamb for a burnt offering."

Then Abraham made an altar, laid the wood upon it, and took Isaac into his arms, and laid him for a lamb upon the altar. But just as he was about to slay this beloved victim, God called to him from Heaven. He looked up from the angry mountains to the rolling clouds of dawn, and God said to him, "Lay not thine hand upon the lad, neither do thou anything unto him; for now I know that thou fearest God, seeing thou hast not withheld thy son from Me."

A Voice sounded to him from Heaven

Bedouins of Palestine weaving mats in
the age-old fashion of the people of the
desert.

This was the last trial of Abraham's splendid faith. The rest of his life was calm and happy. He lived to see his son Isaac married to one of his kindred, the beautiful Rebekah; and when he died he was laid by the side of Sarah, in the cave of Machpelah.

Isaac and His Sons

ISAAC, son of Abraham, was married to a woman named Rebekah, and he loved her tenderly. He became a rich man. He not only increased his flocks and herds, but he set himself, in addition, to plow land and grow corn. His courage and his skill helped to make his wealth. When famine came, he did not sit down and mourn, but moved away to more fertile country, and began again.

When his wealth made other people envious, and they stopped up his wells so that his flocks and herds might perish, he quietly set himself to dig other wells and prayed to God for His protection.

God, who had blessed Abraham, blessed his son Isaac, and appeared to him in the midst of his troubles, saying, "I am the God of Abraham thy father; fear not, for I am with thee, and will bless thee, and multiply thy seed for my servant Abraham's sake."

Isaac rested in this promise. His character was so calm and noble, his manner of life so honorable and beautiful, that even those who had sought to do him harm became his friends, and confessed that God had blessed him.

Hebron, 20 miles southwest of Jerusalem, is one of the oldest cities in Biblical history. Abraham once lived here, and it was from Hebron that Joseph set out to find his brethren at Shechem. Mosque (towers, left background) contains cenotaphs of Abraham, Isaac, Jacob, Sarah, Rebecca and Leah, erected above the places where their tombs are presumed to be.

After nineteen years of marriage, Rebekah, his wife, gave birth to two sons, Esau and Jacob. The joy of Isaac was now complete. His farming prospered, his heart was filled with peace, and his sons grew up in health and strength to rejoice the eyes of his age.

Now, these two boys were very different in character. Esau, the elder, was an outdoor lad; he loved riding and hunting, he was strong and powerful, he rejoiced in the splendid and dangerous risks of a wild life. Jacob, on the other hand, was quiet and thoughtful; he was adored by his mother, who kept him at her side, and he preferred thinking to action.

We can imagine how his mother would tell him of his wonderful grandfather, the rich and powerful Abraham, who had seen visions of God, and to whom God had made the promise that his children should be a great nation. Jacob would think much of these things.

Esau probably thought little about Abraham and his dreams. All he cared about were the joy of hunting and the exercise of his bodily strength. In some ways he was a fine character, for he was entirely free from avarice—he did not think how rich he would be when his father died, and he was not proud of being the eldest son and the heir.

He married two wives from the tribe of Hittites, which greatly displeased his father. But Esau did not care. He probably laughed when his father reproved him. And yet we know that in spite of this disobedience Isaac loved his brave, gallant and willful son.

To show how reckless and wild was this bold hunter, he came home one day hot and weary from the chase, and found Jacob preparing a dish of food, the smell of which was very pleasant to him. He asked for it, and Jacob replied that the food should be Esau's if Esau would give him his birthright; and Esau agreed. For a dish of food (a mess of pottage), because he was hungry, he gave up the privilege of being the heir of Isaac.

Such were the characters of these two men. Esau, reckless, careless, but brave and generous; Jacob, gentle and thoughtful, but inclined to cunning.

How Jacob and His Mother Deceived Isaac
and Stole the Birthright

When their father, Isaac, was an old man, and his eyes were dim, he called Esau to his side, and told him to take bow and arrow and go out to shoot venison and return to him with meat, that he might lay his hands upon his elder son and bless him.

Rebekah, mother of Esau and Jacob, heard these words. As soon as Esau had gone out she whispered to Jacob, her favorite, that he should go and kill two kids, and she would make meat of them, and he should carry it to his father and receive the blessing. Jacob listened to his mother and agreed to do as she desired, only saying that he feared to be discovered.

"Behold, Esau my brother is a hairy man, and I am a smooth man! My father peradventure will feel me, and I shall seem to him as a deceiver."

Rebekah dressed him in Esau's clothes, and put the skins of animals on his arms and neck. They both set themselves to deceive the dying, blind, old man.

Jacob carried the meat to his father, and his father was surprised. They spoke together in this manner, the father troubled by suspicion, the son trembling with shame and fear:

ISAAC: Who art thou, my son?

JACOB: I am Esau, thy firstborn; I have done according as thou badest me. Arise, I pray thee, sit and eat of my venison, that thy soul may bless me!

ISAAC: How is it that thou hast found it so quickly, my son?

JACOB: Because the Lord thy God brought it to me.

ISAAC: Come near, I pray thee, that I may feel thee, my son, whether thou be my very son Esau or not. The voice is Jacob's voice, but the hands are the hands of Esau. Art thou my very son Esau?

JACOB: I am.

Thus Jacob received the blessing of Isaac, who smelt the raiment

Closeup view of the Mosque Machpelah at Hebron, burial place of Abraham, Isaac, Jacob and Sarah. (Gen. 23:19-20)

Rebecca at the well—"And the damsel was very fair to look upon . . . and she went down to the well, and filled her pitcher . . ." (Gen. 24:16)

of Esau which Jacob was wearing, and exclaimed with fatherly love, "See, the smell of my son is as the smell of a field which the Lord hath blessed!"

When Jacob had gone out, and Isaac lay alone in the dim chamber, thinking of God's promises to his father, Abraham, and praying that the son whom he had just blessed might receive the guidance of God, lo! there came in to him his true son, Esau, whom he deeply loved.

Isaac said, "Who art thou?"

And he said, "I am thy son, thy firstborn, Esau." And Isaac trembled very exceedingly, and said, "Who? Where is he that hath taken venison and brought it me, and I have eaten of all before thou camest, and have blessed him?"

When Esau heard the words of his father, he cried with a great and bitter cry, and said unto his father, "Bless me, even me also, O my father!"

This scene is one of the most pathetic and beautiful in all the writings of the world. Who can not see the horror in the dying, sightless eyes of the grand old farmer, and the bitter repentance of the reckless son as he knelt there, knowing, too late, that he had squandered his birthright? We can almost hear the sobs of the hunter, and see the trembling of the dying patriarch.

Esau's fury against the brother who had supplanted him was deep

Esau gave his birthright for a dish of food

and terrible. He vowed to kill him. But Rebekah heard of this and, making a pretense that she wished Jacob to marry one of their own people, she persuaded Isaac to let Jacob go to her brother Laban, who lived far away, and there find a wife.

Her purpose was to send Jacob away only till Esau's wrath had vanished; but her purpose was frustrated by the will of God. She had sinned; she had taught Jacob to deceive. Though her act was prompted by love, nevertheless, like every other sin, it had to meet its own punishment; and in kissing her son and sending him away for a few weeks, she was in reality parting from him for ever.

"Art thou my very son Esau?"

Jacob, the Wanderer

JACOB set out from his father's house to escape the anger of his brother Esau, whom he had deceived.

Jacob believed in God. As he went away from his home, and began his long and perilous journey, he must have thought to himself, "I have done a wicked thing. I have deceived my own brother. What does God think of me?"

He was alone, with only his guilty thoughts for companions.

As night came on he drew near the city of Luz; but he was either afraid to enter it or too footsore and broken to go farther. He took some stones, piled them together for a pillow, and then, casting himself down on the ground, composed himself for sleep.

His last thought was surely one of bitter and aching repentance. Yesterday he had been a loved and honored son in the house of his rich father. Tonight he was a wanderer upon the face of the earth.

His repentance, we may be quite certain, was earnest and sincere; and while he slept there came to him a vision. Jacob saw a wonderful golden ladder rising up from the bare rocks of the valley where he lay, reaching up into the glory of Heaven. On this ladder was a great company of angels, some ascending to Heaven, some descending to earth. Even from these bare, cold rocks there was a way to Heaven, and even from Heaven to these bare, cold rocks God sent down the comfort of His love.

While Jacob gazed entranced at this dazzling ladder, there came to him a voice, saying, "I am the Lord God of Abraham thy father, and the God of Isaac," and a promise that He would be with him.

The well in a Palestinian town is important to all its residents. Here, a donkey team is harnessed to raise water from the depths of an ancient well in South Palestine.

The ancient village of Siloah, near Jerusalem, a scene reminiscent of the well where Jacob met Rachel. (Gen. 29:1-12)

Native women of Palestine still fetch water at the well, in the manner used by women hundreds of years earlier.

Refreshed by his vision, Jacob rose up early and went forward on his journey. He knew now that there is forgiveness of sin.

When he had come into "the land of the people of the east," he saw before him shepherds watering their flocks at a well. He came up to them just as they had finished, and had rolled the stone over the mouth of the well. He asked them whence they came; and they said Haran. He asked if they knew a man there named Laban; and they answered yes. "Is he well?" asked Jacob. "He is well," they replied. "And, behold, Rachel, his daughter, cometh with the sheep."

Jacob looked up quickly and saw a beautiful dark maiden approaching him in the golden dust raised by a flock of sheep. This was his cousin, the daughter of his mother's brother. He was amazed by her beauty, and from that instant loved her tenderly. While she was yet a little distance away, he rolled the stone from the well, and waited for her to approach.

Then he told her who he was; and he wept—so weary and sad was he. Rachel bade him be happy, and hurried on to tell her father of his nephew's arrival. Jacob followed, struck by her beauty and sweetness.

Laban, with his two daughters, Leah and Rachel, received Jacob kindly, and made him feel at home in this strange land; and Jacob stayed with Laban as a guest for a month, enjoying the hopitality of his uncle and the society of his beautiful cousin Rachel.

After that time Jacob offered to work for Laban, and Laban accepted his services. But what wages should he pay his nephew? Jacob answered, "I will serve thee seven years for Rachel, thy younger daughter." And Laban agreed.

Jacob loved Rachel with a noble and heroic love. No longer did he think of returning to his home in a few days. He was content to wait in this strange land, that he might win Rachel. At last the day broke when the wanderer, now a changed and upright man, was to receive his bride.

Laban prepared a fine feast, and invited many friends and relatives to witness the occasion.

65

Rachel's tomb, near Bethlehem, visited
and revered by both Jews and Moslems.
The key to the tomb is in the custody of
Jerusalem's chief rabbi.

Somewhere near this point where it is possible to wade across the Jabbok River, Jacob spent a night in which he met God "face to face." (Gen. 32:22-32)

We can imagine the feelings of this noble man, who had toiled hard for seven years, when Laban advanced toward him leading by the hand the veiled figure of his bride. But when the marriage ceremony was over, and the veil was lifted from the bride, Jacob saw that he had married not Rachel, but Leah. Laban made light of his

disappointment, and said churlishly that in that country it was not proper for the younger daughter to wed before the older.

"If you would have Rachel for your second wife," he said, "you must serve another seven years."

Jacob's love for Rachel was so great that he submitted to Laban's cruel order. It was permitted to men to have more than one wife in those days, and Jacob promised to serve seven more years because of his desire to win the beautiful Rachel.

So Rachel became his wife and Jacob was happy. After the second seven years of service, Jacob longed to take his family to the home of his childhood.

Jacob succeeded finally in coming to an arrangement with Laban, and then with his wives and servants, and his flocks and herds,

Jacob followed, struck by her beauty and sweetness

made his great journey to the west. What a sight that must have been—the cavalcade of the wanderer returning to his old home!

As he drew nearer and nearer to this loved home, he became oppressed by the fear that Esau's anger might yet burn hotly against him. Therefore he sent messengers ahead to tell Esau of his coming.

These messengers returned saying that Esau was advancing at the head of four hundred men. Jacob was afraid, and sent forward more messengers with presents for Esau. After that he assisted his wives and sons, and all the company, to cross the ford called Jabbok, and then withdrew to pray.

On the morrow the sun shone upon Jacob, and there was joy in his heart as he hurried forward to rejoin the cavalcade, for he felt that God had blessed him.

When he encountered Esau, his brother, instead of angry words and blows between them, there were warm words and kisses, and Jacob declared his repentance before all the company.

With Jacob, whose name we must henceforth call Israel—one of the mightiest names in the world—was his little son Joseph, the son of the lovely Rachel. Another son, Benjamin, soon after was born to Rachel, but at his birth Rachel died, and Israel was heartbroken. Yet he found comfort in his sons, particularly in Rachel's sons, Joseph and little Benjamin, and these brothers grew up in love.

Joseph, the Dreamer

ISRAEL had twelve sons; but he loved Joseph, the son of his beloved Rachel, more than any other of his children. The old man took pleasure in making his favorite child a grand coat, which was so royal in its bright colors that his brothers became angry and jealous.

Joseph dreamed strange dreams; and told them to his father and his brothers. He could not explain to them what those dreams meant, but the father and the brothers saw plainly their significance. "Shalt thou indeed reign over us?" cried his older brothers, and they hated him.

One day Israel sent Joseph on an errand to his brothers who were watching the sheep in a distant field. As Joseph drew near to them one of the brothers said bitterly, "Behold this dreamer cometh!" Then they plotted and agreed to kill him. But Reuben, one of the brothers, pleaded for Joseph, and said: "Shed no blood, but cast him into this pit." Secretly in his heart the good Reuben determined to rescue Joseph. So they took Joseph, stripped him of his coat, and flung him into the pit.

Later, at a moment when Reuben was not with the other brothers, a company of Ishmaelites came by, on camels, carrying spices into Egypt. One of the brothers suggested that Joseph should be sold as a slave to these merchants. He was lifted out of the pit, and sold for twenty pieces of silver, and carried away. When Reuben returned and found that he was too late to save Joseph, he was very sad. The other brothers killed a kid, dipped Joseph's coat in the blood, and carried it to their father. When Israel saw it he cried

Jacob's well is located on a plot of land which he purchased "for a hundred lambs" (Gen. 33:19-20). It was here that Joseph's brothers sold him into slavery.

that an evil beast had devoured Joseph. When the others would have comforted him he put them by, saying:

"I shall go down into the grave unto my son, mourning."

Joseph in Egypt

Joseph, in the meantime, had been taken from the land of Canaan to Egypt, and sold by the merchants. He became a servant to the captain of the king's guard. Here he prospered, and Potiphar, his master, trusted him, and loved him. But Potiphar's wife hated Joseph, because, when she tempted him to do a dishonorable thing, he remained faithful to his master and friend. So this wretched woman lied against Joseph to Potiphar, and Potiphar, believing her, had Joseph cast into prison.

In the prison the keeper became his friend, and he made Joseph an overseer of the other prisoners. Now, in this prison were two servants of the great king of Egypt, Pharaoh, and they told him of some strange dreams they had had, and Joseph declared what those dreams meant. One of the servants, he said, would shortly be restored to the King's favor. The other would soon die.

Both these predictions came true; and one day, when Pharaoh was troubled by an evil dream, the servant who had been restored to his favor remembered Joseph, and spoke of him to the King. Then Joseph was brought out of prison, and told the King the meaning of his dream. For seven years, he said, God would bless the land of Egypt with overflowing harvests; and after that for seven years, Egypt should suffer from drought and famine. Let Pharaoh learn of God, he said, and put over the land a man who would hoard the corn of the years of plenty, so that the people might not die in the years of famine.

Pharaoh took off his ring and put it on Joseph's hand, and arrayed him in fine linen, and put a gold chain about his neck, and made him ride in the second chariot and made him governor over all the land of Egypt.

A camel caravan skirts the shores of the Mediterranean, following the ancient trade route from the Holy Land to Egypt.

Joseph was taken to Egypt and sold

While Joseph governed in great glory and honor, there came, as he had prophesied, a bitter famine, and his old father, Israel, hearing that there was corn in the barns of Egypt, sent his sons to purchase the precious grain from the Egyptians. He sent all his sons, except the last-born, Benjamin, fearing that some evil might befall his favorite.

Can you not picture to yourself the moving scene when those ten sons of Israel, strangers from a far country, stood before the mighty governor under Pharaoh, and knew not that he was their own brother, the dreamer whom they had sold into bondage? Joseph knew the land they came from and recognized them as his brothers. He steeled his heart against them, however, and treated them with suspicion, as if he thought them to be spies, enemies of his country.

74

He allowed them to fill their sacks with corn, received their money from them, but insisted that Simeon, one of the brothers, should remain with him while the others returned home and brought Benjamin to him.

On their way home the nine brothers discovered that the money they had paid for the corn was wrapped up in their sacks; and they began to be afraid of a new disaster. Israel, their father, when he heard that Benjamin was demanded, burst into lamentation, and would not let him go. But the corn began to run low, and when starvation was staring them in the face once more, the brothers persuaded the old father to let his youngest son go with them into Egypt.

75

Joseph's ten brothers probably travelled along this
dusty caravan road, main thoroughfare between Egypt
and Palestine, when they went to buy corn in Egypt
during a great famine. (Gen. 42:3)

The famed pyramids of Gizeh at twilight along the Nile, a scene familiar even to Joseph. Numbered among the "Seven Wonders of the World," the pyramids are the only ones which have survived intact.

Once again the brothers stood before the great governor. This time Joseph looked on the little son of his mother Rachel, the little brother he had loved so dearly. The brothers bowed themselves to the ground and presented their gifts to Joseph. "Is your father well?" he said graciously. "The old man of whom ye spake—is he yet alive?" And they answered, "Thy servant, our father, is in good health, he is yet alive." And they bowed down their heads and made obeisance.

Then Joseph, mastering the love that was breaking his heart, turned and looked at Benjamin. The sight was greater than he could bear. All the past rushed to his eyes in "the water of the soul." He withdrew quickly into a private room and burst into tears. Afterward, when he had washed his face and recovered his composure, he returned to the brothers and invited them to eat with him. Greatly astonished, they sat down to eat, and their astonishment increased when they saw that the mighty governor, who sat at the high table by himself, sent the richest of his dishes to Benjamin. They were returning home early in the morning when one of Joseph's officers overtook them, and accused them of stealing his

The brothers bowed themselves to the ground

master's silver cup. The sacks were opened, and in the mouth of Benjamin's sack lay the missing vessel. The brothers all returned to Joseph, and prostrated themselves before him in great fear. Joseph said they might return in peace, all except Benjamin, in whose sack the cup had been found; he must remain and become his servant. Then one of the brothers stood up and said:

"Oh, my lord, let thy servant, I pray thee, speak a word in my lord's ear, and let not thine anger burn against thy servant, for thou art even as Pharaoh. My lord asked his servants, saying, 'Have ye a father or a brother?' And we said unto my lord, 'We have a father, an old man, and a child of his old age, a little one; and his brother is dead, and he alone is left of his mother, and his father loveth him.'

"And thou saidst unto thy servants, Bring him down unto me, that I may set mine eyes upon him.' And we said unto my lord, 'The lad can not leave his father: for if he should leave his father, his father would die.' And thou saidst unto thy servants, 'Except your youngest brother come down with you, ye shall see my face no more.'

"And it came to pass when we came up unto thy servant, my father, we told him the words of my lord. And thy servant, my father, said unto us, 'Ye know that my wife bare me two sons: and the one went out from me, and I said, "Surely he is torn in pieces." And I saw him not since. And if ye take this also from me, and mischief befall him, ye shall bring down my gray hairs with sorrow to the grave. "

Joseph could not bear any longer the sorrow of this appeal. Hastily he dismissed his retinue of servants, and stood alone in the great hall with his brothers. Then he bowed his head and wept as a strong man weeps when he is stricken to the soul. And while his brothers marveled to see this powerful governor in tears, he raised his head, and exclaimed, "I am Joseph!"

He made no reproach to them for their first cruelty, and bade them not to reproach themselves. He told them to hasten back to Canaan, to tell Israel that Joseph was yet alive, and to bring their father, and all their people, to Egypt. And after he had said these kind things he went forward to his brother Benjamin, the playmate of his childhood, and kissed him.

Pharaoh heard of this beautiful scene, and rejoiced again in Joseph. He sent wagons and rich presents to old Israel in Canaan, and bade him come down to live in Egypt. And Israel, the old, old man, who had once slept with stones for his pillow, had but one cry when he heard all this greatness: "Joseph, my son, is yet alive! I will go and see him before I die!"

Joseph Honors His Father

Joseph drove out in his chariot to meet his father, and they met on the frontier of Egypt—the old man and the young governor. And we are told that Joseph "presented himself unto him," and he fell on his neck and wept. And Israel said to Joseph, "Now let me die, since I have seen thy face, because thou art yet alive."

Then Israel stood before Pharaoh and blessed the mighty King, and he settled in the land of Goshen and Joseph cared for him, and the Israelites flourished exceedingly. Israel's death, after his long life of wandering, was full of peace.

At the death of their father, Joseph's brothers feared Joseph's wrath, thinking that now he would surely take revenge on them. But Joseph had no such thoughts in his great soul, and he comforted them and spake kindly unto them.

And so the dreamer's dreams came true. And when Joseph died at a great age, he saw not only his greatness equal with Pharaoh's; he saw his children's children, to the third generation, living in prosperity among the Egyptians.

"I die," said Joseph, "and God will surely visit you, and bring you out of this land into the land which He promised to Abraham, to Isaac, and to Jacob."

The Rise of Moses in Egypt

YEARS went on. The Israelites grew rich and happy and numerous among the Egyptians. At length there came a time when a king reigned over Egypt who knew nothing at all about Joseph. This mighty Pharaoh, sitting on his throne, listened to the complaints of his Egyptian counselors, who could not bear the thought of the Israelites, foreigners, growing rich in Egypt. So the Pharaoh himself came to consider the foreign Israelites first a nuisance, and then a danger to his kingdom.

81

Pharaoh set himself to break the spirit of these proud foreigners. By a word of command, the great Pharaoh made the whole host of these prosperous Israelites the slaves of his will. They were driven from their homes and their belongings were taken from them. They were formed into gangs, and marched away under taskmasters, who lashed them with whips, to make bricks for Pharaoh's new cities. The once happy Israelite, laughing and content in the midst of his family, became a flogged and bleeding slave, toiling under a burning sun without wages and without hope.

But such was the quiet endurance of these Israelites that even as slaves, and in the midst of a life so hard and cruel and hopeless, they grew in numbers, and showed a cheerful face to their oppressors. Pharaoh, seeing how they still increased, gave the abominable order that every boy born to an Israelite should be instantly killed. The people ordered to carry out this command refused, and then Pharoah gave the order that the boy children should be thrown into the Nile. Many a poor Israelitish mother must have tried to hide her baby from the cruel Egyptians! What plotting and planning there must have been to hide the birth of boy babies!

The princess spied the ark

Among these mothers was a woman named Jochebed, who had a baby boy. This boy was extremely beautiful, and the mother determined to do everything in her power to save him from the Egyptian murderers. For more than three months she managed to conceal him, and then, fearing that the spies would discover her secret, she set about a very original plan of saving him. She made a little ark, or cradle, of papyrus, coated it with pitch, and put her baby carefully within it; then she placed this baby's boat among the bulrushes of the Nile, and set her daughter Miriam to watch from afar and see what happened.

Miriam presently beheld a company of noble Egyptian ladies approaching the river, and knew that among them was the princess of Egypt, the daughter of the mighty Pharaoh. The princess, walk-

ing beside the river, spied the ark floating on the water, and bade one of her maidens fetch it. The order was obeyed, and the ladies crowded round the princess as the ark was presented to her. When the lid was raised, and before the ladies could utter an exclamation of surprise, the beautiful little baby opened his eyes and burst into tears. This touched the princess to the heart, and, though she knew the baby to be an Israelite, she determined to rear him and keep him at her side. While they were all bending over the baby and admiring him, Miriam approached, and, hearing what the princess said, asked whether she should go and fetch a nurse to rear the baby. The princess agreed, and off went Miriam to fetch her mother, who rejoiced to know that her boy was safe, and that once again she could nurse him.

Pharaoh's daughter called the baby Moses, which means saved from water, and took the greatest pains with his education. The little Israelite was trained by the wisest of the Egyptian teachers, and grew up in Pharaoh's palace amidst all the luxury and refinement and learning of a great court. But, although he grew up among Egyptians, he remained deep in his heart an Israelite, and his blood burned like a fire in his veins whenever he saw the cruelties under which his people groaned. One day, when he was a grown man, the sight of an Israelite being flogged by a taskmaster so worked upon the mind of Moses that, thinking himself unobserved, he went forward and slew the taskmaster. Some time after this he sought to persuade two quarreling Israelites to "make it up"; but, instead of doing this, they turned on him, and taunted him with having murdered an Egyptian. Moses became frightened. He knew that if the murder was disclosed to the authorities he would certainly be killed. Therefore he fled from Egypt and took service with Jethro, the chief of the Hebrew people in Midian.

In this pleasant country Moses dwelt for many years. It must have seemed to him that his strange and romantic life had now settled down to peace and quiet domestic happiness. He married one of Jethro's daughters, and tended his father-in-law's flocks, dwelling much among the vast, silent spaces of nature, where God's peace seemed to rest.

But Moses could never forget the awful sights he had seen in Egypt. Again and again the vision rose before his eyes of gangs of almost naked Israelites making bricks under a burning sun, while the lashes of the taskmasters' whips hissed through the air and tore at their straining bodies. The injustice and cruelty embittered his thoughts.

It happened that one day, as he was watching Jethro's flocks close by a mountain, he saw a bush on fire, and, going toward it, he observed, to his amazement, that although the fire blazed all round and through the bush, yet the bush was not consumed. He went nearer, and then God called to him out of the midst of the fire. Moses, so frightened that he knew not what to say, answered the God who called him by name; and God then bade him take off his shoes, for the ground on which he stood was holy. Then did the shepherd realize that he was in a sacred place, and, taking off his shoes and covering his face, he waited in great fear to hear what God would say.

God spoke out of the burning bush and said:

"I have surely seen the affliction of My people which are in Egypt, and have heard their cry by reason of their taskmasters; for I know their sorrows. . . . Come now, therefore, and I will send thee unto Pharaoh, that thou mayst bring forth My people the children of Israel out of Egypt."

Moses asked what he should say to the children of Israel if they demanded of him: What is the name of thy God?

Then God said words which have a wonderful meaning for us, a greater meaning than they could ever have had for Moses: "Thus shalt thou say unto the children, Jehovah hath sent me unto you."

Moses was afraid, and sought to escape this duty. But he was at last persuaded, and God told him that his brother Aaron should go with him to stand before Pharaoh; and that although Pharaoh would refuse to let the Israelites go, yet in the end, by the might of God's hand, Pharaoh should be bound, and the Israelites go free.

And Moses, although reluctantly, accepted the duty laid upon him, and forsook his flocks and herds, and gave up the quiet peace of his life, and in his old age went forward on the greatest and most momentous journey that ever fell to the lot of mortal man.

When Moses knew that it was the will of God that he should go back to Egypt and deliver his oppressed nation from the terrible slavery of Pharaoh, he no longer hesitated and argued with himself, but set out, with his family and with Aaron, his brother, for the land where the Israelites toiled. Here the two brothers gathered the people together and declared to them the will of God. Imagine the joy of this once rich and prosperous and happy people, who had been degraded by Pharaoh to the meanest slavery, when they heard that God had sent Moses and Aaron to deliver them out of the hand of Pharaoh and give them a country of their own!

Moses went forward again, strong in the gratitude of his people, and stood before the mighty King of Egypt. Pharaoh listened to the Hebrew's words with a sneer. The God of the Hebrews was nothing to him. He despised the people and their God.

To show Moses how little he cared for his strong words, Pharaoh gave orders that the straw which hitherto had been provided for the Hebrews at their brickmaking should be gathered by themselves, and yet that the taskmaster should see that the number of bricks made each day was the same. Under this new tyranny the spirit of the Israelites broke, and their hearts grew furious against Moses and Aaron.

"What have you done but add to our burdens?" they cried bitterly.

Moses bade them have patience. He said that Pharaoh had refused to believe the words of God; now he should know what this God of Israel could do. Moses calmly and quietly set himself against the tyrant king in this strange land, sure in the knowledge that God would deliver His people.

Moses stood before Pharaoh and showed him by marvelous deeds that he did indeed speak for the invisible God, to Whom nothing is impossible. But Pharaoh laughed, thinking that Moses and Aaron were but clever conjurers. Then Moses warned him that God would certainly send signs to Pharaoh—signs many and terrible of His wrath and indignation—but Pharaoh only laughed, and would not let the people of Israel go free.

The warning of Moses came true. Egypt was smitten by the displeasure of God. Ten great plagues fell upon the land. Her lovely waters became red like blood; a multitude of frogs spread themselves across the land, and died in vast heaps, so that the air stank; the dust became a heaving, creeping swarm of lice, which settled upon man and beast; flies rose up in the air and descended upon the houses, entering in at doors and windows, and blackening all the color and glory of man's art; a fearful disease broke out among the cattle of the Egyptians, so that they died; the people of Pharaoh were afflicted with boils and blisters, corrupting their bodies and destroying their peace; thunder rolled about the land, the heavens opened, and a storm of pitiless hail beat upon the crops, broke even the branches of great trees, and made desolate the whole land; locusts, greater in size than had ever been before, so numerous that they darkened all the land, now marched like an invincible army across the country, destroying everything over which they passed; darkness, blacker than blackest night—a thick darkness, a darkness which might be felt—descended out of heaven and steeped the land of Egypt in its gloom; and, last of all, and more terrible than all, the angel of the Lord passed through the land of Egypt and smote the eldest child of all the Egyptians, from the first-born of Pharaoh himself to the first-born of the prisoners in the dungeon.

Then Pharaoh rose up in the night, he and all his servants, and all the Egyptians; and there was a great cry in Egypt, for there was not a house where there was not one dead.

Now the mourning and brokenhearted Egyptians were eager for the Israelites to go, and they cried to Pharaoh that he should send the slaves away, and Pharaoh ordered Moses and Aaron to gather the Israelites together and to depart immediately.

With great rejoicing the Israelites came together in a mighty host, and, with Moses and Aaron to guide them, set out on the march to Canaan.

Moses and the children of Israel are said to have encamped here on the shores of the Red Sea, while enroute from Mount Sinai to conquer the Promised Land, Canaan. (Num. 33:35)

The tyrant King bade Moses take his people and go

Now, to avoid a nation that might have afflicted them again, they went not by a straight route to the Promised Land, but by a great curve, and it is that curve of the Israelites which remains for all ages as one of the most wonderful marches in the story of mankind.

God led His people in a wonderful way. By day a pillar of cloud went before the marching host, and by night a pillar of fire. It came to pass that as they drew near the banks of the Red Sea, rejoicing in their deliverance, and delighting greatly in the prospect of a new country where they would be free and happy and prosperous, suddenly a noise from behind broke upon them.

Turning about, the Israelites beheld the chariots and horsemen of Pharaoh approaching them in battle array. In an instant the host of Israel was thrown into confusion. First they called upon Moses to save them and then they bitterly upbraided him for delivering them out of slavery only to have them fall at the hand of the sword. But Moses quieted the terrors of these foolish and ungrateful pilgrims, whose courage and manhood had been broken by years of tyranny. He bade them trust in God, and remember the plagues which had afflicted Pharaoh. Then God spoke and said, "Speak unto the children of Israel that they go forward."

The pillar of cloud stood between the Israelites and Pharaoh's host, and Moses, going forward, stretched out his hands over the sea, and a great wind arose which blew all night, and divided the waters. So the children of Israel went into the midst of the sea upon the dry ground; and the waters were a wall on their right hand and on their left.

But when Pharaoh's host entered the sea in pursuit of the Israelites, the wheels of the chariots stuck fast in the sand. A frightful confusion broke out among them, and in the midst of that host of plunging horses and shouting soldiers, the walls of water fell with deafening clamor, and the host of Pharaoh perished in the sea. The Israelites, standing on the farther bank, when they beheld that new miracle of God, and realized that now at last they were free, broke into songs of thanksgiving; and Miriam took a timbrel in her hand, and all the women joined her with timbrels and with dances.

The March in the Desert

NEVER in all the story of the world has there been a march so romantic, so wonderful, and so full of meaning for the rest of mankind as the great march made by the Israelites under the leadership of Moses.

Think of the spectacle! Through the wild country which lies on the farther side of the Red Sea went a whole nation. Husbands and wives, fathers and mothers, brothers and sisters, boys and girls, children scarcely able to walk, and babes at their mothers' breasts. For an immense distance stretched this extraordinary caravan, this multitude of humanity. And remember, always remember, that this nation trekking across the wilderness had been weakened almost to dust and ashes by slavery. Their manhood had been flogged out of them by the whips of Pharaoh's taskmasters.

For centuries they had sweated on the red dust of Egypt, under the pitiless glare of the Egyptian sun, despised, scorned by the people over them, hopeless of any change in their condition, and powerless to strike a blow in defense of themselves or their wives and children. It sounded like an idle tale in their ears that once long ago, in the days of Joseph, they had been a free, great and mighty people in the land of Egypt. Remember, then, that this huge caravan was a poor bedraggled host of querulous slaves, whose backs were still raw from the whips of their tyrants, and whose souls were still cowed with the fear of their despots.

For three rainless days this ragged multitude streamed across the desert, now elated by their escape from slavery, and now plunged into despair at the unending waste of land always before them. We can surely hear with the ears of our imagination the

The unending waste of land into which
Moses led the Israelites after their flight
from Egypt can be clearly seen in this
landscape of the Negev Desert in the
southernmost part of Israel.

The rugged terrain of the Negev Desert of Israel is transversed by a tortuous road leading south to the Gulf of Akkaba and the Red Sea.

This rock, in ancient Edom, is said to be the one which Moses struck with his rod to bring forth water, to satisfy the thirst of the children of Israel and their cattle. (Num. 20:7-13)

groans of the old and the murmurings of the young, as Moses marched steadily forward into this burning and waterless land. After all, some of them must have thought, it was better to make bricks for Pharaoh than to die of thirst in the wilderness.

The air of that long-silent desert must have been continuously loud with the increasing murmurs of the Hebrews. And when at length water did appear, and the people rushed forward with a wild excitement to drink, lo! it was so bitter that they murmured against Moses. Moses must have guessed to the full at the waters of Marah (which means bitterness) the terrible difficulties of his task. It is often hard for a king or a statesman to keep a prosperous people happy, but Moses was alone with a horde of miserable slaves in a strange and desolate country.

Guided by God, this truly great and farseeing captain took a tree that grew near the bitter waters, and threw it into their midst. The waters immediately became good to drink. Then the thirsty people drank, and went forward once again, till they came to a place of much water and many palm trees, where they rested, and were glad.

Once again they plunged into the desert, and soon hunger drove them into more murmuring against Moses and Aaron. "Would to God," they cried, "we had died by the hand of the Lord in Egypt, when we sat by the fleshpots, and when we did eat bread to the full; for ye have brought us forth into this wilderness to kill the whole assembly with hunger."

Some of them took up stones to kill Moses, but he rebuked them, and drew water for them from a rock. And while they drank, and rested in this place, which is called Rephidim, suddenly a warlike body of a tribe called the Amalekites appeared in the distance.

How Joshua Fought the Amalekites

Moses called to his side a warlike young man named Joshua, and bade him go out with a picked body of the Israelites to meet the Amalekites. And while Joshua did his bidding, Moses went up with Aaron and Hur to the top of a hill, "and it came to pass when Moses held up his hand that Israel prevailed; and when he let down his hand, Amalek prevailed. But Moses' hands were heavy, and they took a stone, and put it under him, and he sat thereon, and Aaron and Hur stayed up his hands, and his hands were steady until the going down of the sun. And Joshua discomfited Amalek and his people with the edge of the sword."

Moses received at Rephidim a visit from his father-in-law, Jethro, who had heard the wonderful news of the Israelites' exodus from Egypt. And Jethro, seeing how Moses was overburdened by the work of leadership, and how he had to sit in judgment in any little dispute between these quarrelsome people, said to Moses, "Thou wilt surely wear away . . . this thing is too heavy for thee; thou art not able to perform it thyself."

And this wise old man bade Moses choose from the people, "able men, such as fear God, men of truth, hating covetousness; and place such over them, to be rulers of thousands, and rulers of hundreds, rulers of fifties, and rulers of tens; and let them judge the people at all seasons; and it shall be that every great matter they shall bring unto thee, but every small matter they shall judge: so shall it be easier for thyself, and they shall bear the burden with thee."

This wonderful talk of Jethro with Moses might be called the beginning of politics. Politics is the science in which men study how they should arrange the laws of a nation so that people may grow in virtue, prosperity, and happiness. This conversation of Moses with his father-in-law interests us exceedingly, because the first step in social reform was made in those far-off days, and has been followed and developed by almost every nation since.

The march was continued. The mighty caravan, flushed by their victory over the Amalekites, and dreaming great dreams of Canaan, pushed across the desert and halted under the shadow of Mount Sinai. Moses was called by God into the mountain, and there, in the midst of a great cloud, received the ten great commands of God which are the foundation of all law and all honor.

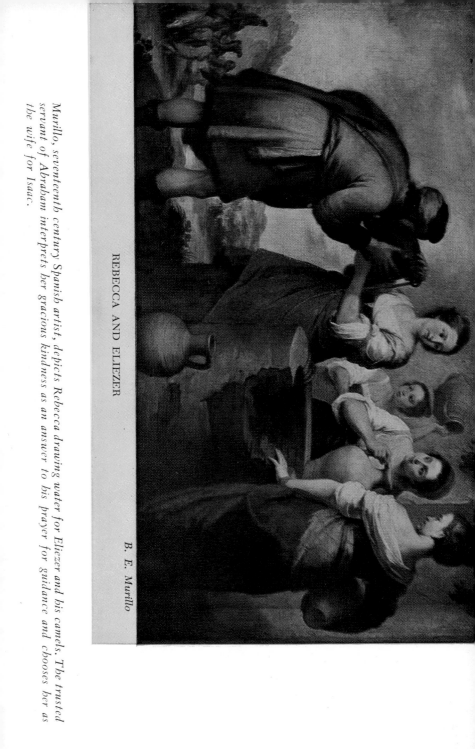

REBECCA AND ELIEZER

B. E. Murillo

Murillo, seventeenth century Spanish artist, depicts Rebecca drawing water for Eliezer and his camels. The trusted servant of Abraham interprets her gracious kindness as an answer to his prayer for guidance and chooses her as the wife for Isaac.

JACOB'S DREAM   *Domenico Feti*

Jacob, fleeing from Esau's wrath, sleeps in the wilderness with a stone for his pillow and sees angels ascending and descending a ladder from heaven, thus learning that he could not run away from God. The paintings of Domenico Feti, Italian artist who died in 1624, are known for their light and dark contrasts.

Moses received the ten great commands of God

Inside this great mound at Dera'a, southern Syria, is an underground city more
than 3,000 years old. King Og of Bashan,
one of the last of the giants, ruled over
the city. (Deut. 3:11)

So Moses went down from Mount Sinai and gave the people the laws he had received from God.

I. Thou shalt have no other gods before me.

II. Thou shalt not make unto thee any graven image, or any likeness of anything that is in heaven above, or that is in the earth beneath, or that is in the water under the earth:

Thou shalt not bow down thyself to them, nor serve them: for I the Lord thy God am a jealous God, visiting the iniquity of the fathers upon the children unto the third and fourth generation of them that hate me;

And shewing mercy unto thousands of them that love me, and keep my commandments.

III. Thou shalt not take the name of the Lord thy God in vain; for the Lord will not hold him guiltless that taketh his name in vain.

IV. Remember the sabbath day to keep it holy.

Six days shalt thou labor, and do all thy work:

But the seventh day is the sabbath of the Lord thy God: in it thou shalt not do any work, thou, nor thy son, nor thy daughter, thy manservant, nor thy maidservant, nor thy cattle, nor thy stranger that is within thy gates:

For in six days the Lord made heaven and earth, the sea, and all that in them is, and rested the seventh day: wherefore the Lord blessed the sabbath day, and hallowed it.

V. Honor thy father and thy mother: that thy days may be long upon the land which the Lord thy God giveth thee.

VI. Thou shalt not kill.

VII. Thou shalt not commit adultery.

VIII. Thou shalt not steal.

IX. Thou shalt not bear false witness against thy neighbor.

X. Thou shalt not covet thy neighbor's house, thou shalt not covet thy neighbor's wife, nor his manservant, nor his maidservant, nor his ox, nor his ass, nor any thing that is thy neighbor's.

99

These great laws, which seem so simple and right to us, were no
so simple to the Israelites. When Moses descended from the moun
tain he found that his people had disobeyed the chief of them, b
persuading Aaron to make them an image of the golden calf wor
shiped in Egypt as a symbol of God. Thus, while God, who is
Spirit and can be worshiped only in spirit, was so very close to th
host that the mountain where He appeared to Moses burned witl
smoke before their eyes, these poor, foolish, craven people desirec
an outward and visible sign of Him in the shape of a golden calf

The Breaking of the Tables of Stone

So indignant was Moses that he threw down the tables of stone
hurled the golden calf into a fire, and killed the guilty makers o
the idol. Then he returned to the mountain, learned still more o
God's laws for humanity, and received the Almighty's forgivenes
for the sins of the Israelites.

For more than a year the Israelites were encamped under the
shadow of Mount Sinai. There they built a movable temple, with
its Holy of Holies containing an oblong chest, called the Ark o
the Covenant, wherein reposed the two tables of stone on which
the ten commandments were written. Here the sons of Aaron were
chosen as priests, and Aaron himself became the high priest of the
nation. The feasts of the Hebrews were instituted at this place,
and worship was celebrated in a manner to remind the Israelites
of God's great mercy and kindness.

The First Sight of the Promised Land
That the People Could Not Enter

When at last the mighty host moved on once more toward Canaan,
the Israelites again broke into murmurings and complaints concerning the shortness of food. Food was given to them in abundance,
and they ate of it so greedily that many died and were buried in a

An ancient race of giants once dwelled in
these chalky limestone caves near Beit Jibrin.
Inside, the caves have rooms forty feet high,
with oversized olive presses and cisterns still
remaining. (Num. 13:33)

place called The Graves of Lust.

Thus warned, they proceeded on their way, and presently Moses was near enough to the Promised Land to send forward his spies. These men returned with two tales. First, that the land was rich, fruitful, and altogether desirable; and, second, that it was occupied by mighty people, who would fight for it.

The Israelites were at first eager to push on to the wonderful Promised Land. But they were so fearful of fighting that they broke out into violent murmurings against Moses and Aaron. Then God declared to Moses that He would punish the people; that, save Joshua and Caleb, none of that generation should enter the Promised Land. He bade them to return once more to the wilderness, and when some of them disobeyed this command, and went forward to look at the goodly land they had feared to enter, a company of Canaanites and Amalekites fell upon them and smote them back.

In the wilderness a fresh trouble arose. A conspiracy came to light. Three important men, Korah, Dathan and Abiram, with the support of many others, charged Moses and Aaron with taking too much upon themselves. God answered these people and broke the rebellion, but Moses and Aaron began to despair of ever making a great and victorious people of these Israelites. Once, when God commanded him to give the people water from a rock, by calling upon it to flow in His name, Moses contemptuously twice struck the rock with his rod, and spoke harshly to the people.

For many years, wearisome and fretful, the Israelites remained in the wilderness. There Aaron died. The death of this great and noble leader staggered the Israelites, and for thirty days they mourned him sincerely, feeling that something of their past had perished. But a few days after their mourning, coming into a barren waste of land, they once more murmured against God, and were the same bitter, suspicious and quarrelsome people as before. Then from the rocks came little fiery serpents, which stung them so that many died; but when they repented, Moses was commanded by God to make a bronze serpent and to fix it on a pole, and all who looked upon it were healed.

The Moabite Stone, discovered on Mount Nebo during archaelogical excavations. Dated about 890 B.C., it records how King Mesha of Moab seized the mountain to satisfy blood revenge, killing "7,000 men, boys, women and girls" of an Israelite settlement and dedicating his prey to the god Ashtar-Chemosh.

And now it seemed as if the Israelites had learned their lesson. Across their line of march lay many cities, and against these people, who refused to let them pass, they went up stout-heartedly in battle, under the captaincy of Joshua and trusting in God.

Battle after battle ended in triumph for the Israelites, city after city fell before them, and they went forward, no longer a rabble of beaten and grumbling slaves, but a terrible people, inspired by faith in One Invisible God; pure and manly, brave and resolute.

They had now reached the frontier of a territory occupied by the Moabites. The King of the Moabites, whose name was Balak, became so fearful of the Israelites, whose victories were spreading terror through the country, that he sought to stay their progress by magic. He sent to a famous prophet named Balaam, and begged him to come and put a curse upon these invading Israelites. But Balaam found that God would not put a curse in his mouth. However, Balak sent to him again, and with such tempting offers that at last Balaam consented to come; but he protested that he could only utter whatsoever words God put in his mouth.

Balaam, the False Prophet, Rides on His Ass to Meet Israel

And as Balaam rode upon his ass the angel of God stood in his way, and the ass saw it and stopped, and Balaam smote the ass. Again the angel appeared, and the ass, starting to one side, crushed Balaam's foot against a wall. Balaam struck it again, and suddenly the ass spoke in human language, and the eyes of Balaam saw the angel. And the angel warned Balaam that he should speak only those words which God put into his mouth.

So Balaam went forward, and was received by King Balak with great honor. He was taken to a high hill overlooking the host of Israelites, and seven altars were erected there, and a bullock and a ram were sacrificed on each altar. But Balaam refused to lay a curse upon the Israelites. Instead, gazing upon the tents of Israel, the

From atop the wind-swept summit of
Mount Nebo, a Palestinian shades his
eyes to view the "Promised Land." This
is the location where "the Lord showed
him" (Moses) the Land of Canaan.
(Deut. 34:1)

spirit of God came upon him, and he cried, "How goodly are thy tents, O Jacob, and thy tabernacles, O Israel!"

But when the spirit passed away from him, Balaam loitered among the Midianites, another tribe, with evil thoughts. He could not bring himself to curse Israel: he dared not do that; but he greatly longed for Balak's reward. And he tempted the Israelites to join an evil feast, that they might enter into the wickedness all about them.

Alas, great bodies of the Israelites flocked to the heathen feast and rioted with the Midianites, and utterly forgot the laws of God which He had given them for their own happiness and advancement. They fell into the vilest sins, and the anger of God descended upon them. Plague broke out among them. They perished in vast numbers, and Moses hanged the chiefs of unfaithful Israelites. But the Midianites were to suffer too. The faithful of Israel were massed by Phinehas, the son of Eleazar the priest, and he went up against the Midianites, destroyed their cities and their chiefs, took captive their women and children, and slew Balaam.

Moses Views the Promised Land from Mount Nebo, and Dies

This great fight put the Israelites into possession of valuable land, and here the tribes of Reuben and Gad, and half of the fighting tribe of Manasseh, settled down to occupy the country.

And now it came upon the aged Moses that the day of his death was at hand. The veteran lawgiver, whose life had begun so romantically in the palace of Pharaoh, and who had spent all the vigor of his manhood in the wilderness with these unruly Israelites, knew that he was about to die; knew that he would never enter the Promised Land to whose frontier he had so bravely brought his people.

He chose Joshua to take his place as leader. Then from the windy peak of Nebo, he looked out with undimmed eyes upon the goodly land. And he died and was buried by God.

The spring of Moses at the foot of Mount Nebo.

Israel Marches Forward

THE story of the Israelites is now the story of Joshua. The name of this mighty captain who led the people into the Promised Land, whose victories gave them the possession of that beautiful country, is of great interest to us.

As soon as the days of mourning for Moses were over, Joshua made his first great forward move. He crossed the river Jordan, and advanced against the city of Jericho. Jericho was the bastion of western Palestine, and without taking it Joshua could not possibly advance into Canaan. Now the city, set in the midst of palms, was not only very beautiful, but was so walled about as to be almost impregnable. Joshua was one day looking toward the city, and pondering his plan of attack, when a vision came to him of one with a sword in his hand who declared himself to be the prince of the army of Jehovah. From this heavenly visitor Joshua received instructions for the taking of Jericho. "Ye shall compass the city, all ye men of war, and go round about the city once. Thus shalt thou do six days. And seven priests shall bear before the Ark seven trumpets of rams' horns: and the seventh day ye shall compass the city seven times, and the priests shall blow with the trumpets. And it shall come to pass, that when they make a long blast with the ram's horn, and when ye hear the sound of the trumpet, all the people shall shout with a great shout; and the wall of the city shall fall down flat, and the people shall ascend up, every man straight before him."

Thus was Israel taught to have faith in the purpose of God. The walls were to fall in a miraculous manner. And Joshua obeyed the vision.

In a deep valley of the Jordan lie the remains of Canaanite Jericho, which fell before Joshua and the army of Israel. Excavations have verified that the city's walls fell outward, as described in Joshua 7:20.

The people of Jericho, who had heard of the warlike Israelites, must have been amazed as they looked down on the plain to see the Ark carried solemnly and silently round their city walls once every day for six days. Not a word came from the Israelites' lips. But on the seventh day, seven times did the Ark make the circuit of the mighty wall, and as the people of Jericho looked and wondered, the priests blew with their trumpets, and then, for the first time, did Israel speak—speak to the heavens in one victorious shout—and lo! the walls fell with a deafening clangor, and the army of Joshua swept forward and possessed the city.

From that moment the tide of victory rolled forward across the land. Joshua's sword was the avenging angel of God. The wicked peoples of Canaan, living in idolatry and sin, trembled at his advance. City after city fell before him. As the locusts had extended across the land of Egypt, so the Israelites extended across the land of Canaan. Nothing could stay their advance. Their very name was a terror in the ears of the Canaanites, and men questioned themselves as to this new God of the Hebrews, called Jehovah.

But there was living in northern Palestine a mighty chief named Jabin, who had all the courage of the north. Jabin set himself to drive out these troublesome Israelites, who had conquered only the weaker peoples of the south. So he gathered a vast army together and came marching down in great strength and splendor against the advancing Israelites.

Joshua heard of their coming, and, swift in action, he massed his army, hurried forward like the wind, and, before Jabin suspected his approach, came down upon him and utterly demolished the northern army. It was this splendid feat of arms which practically decided the whole campaign of conquest. A long and dreary war of several years followed upon the defeat of Jabin, but from the moment of that defeat the fate of the country was really sealed. The miserable and broken-spirited slaves of Pharaoh, who had hungered and starved in the deserts, who had threatened to murder Moses and Aaron, who had more than once abandoned God to worship images, had now become a majestic nation, whose sword was ter-

The walls fell with a deafening clangor

rible. They had at last a country of their own.

The long march was over. The hunger and thirsting were at an end. Forgotten were the old fear of Pharaoh's chariot wheels pursuing from behind and the rattle of the Canaanitish spears advancing toward them. Proudly their young men looked upon a smiling country which was their own, and their women gladly sang the national songs of praise and thanksgiving.

But the old soldier, Joshua, the son of Nun, knew that there still dwelt in this land people who hated the Israelites. True, the Israelites had conquered the country, and, true, they occupied it. Nevertheless, all about them lay people unsubdued, who, peaceful enough now, and fearful of these fighting Israelites, might wait their hour and smite when long peace had loosened the muscles and rusted the spears of the people of God.

Therefore, the last act of Joshua, when he found the invincible enemy Death marching upon his own brave heart, was to summon the people of Israel before him and to remind them of their destiny. "Fear the Lord," said this great soldier, "and serve Him in sincerity and in truth." And the people said they would serve the Lord, who had brought them out of Egypt: "God forbid that we should forsake the Lord to serve other gods; for the Lord our God, He it is that brought us out of the land of Egypt, from the house of bondage." But Joshua was not convinced of his fickle people's sincerity. He raised a stone, and set it under an oak that was by the sanctuary, and said to the people, "Behold, this stone shall be a witness unto us; for it hath heard all the words of the Lord which He spake unto us; it shall be therefore a witness unto you, lest ye deny your God."

Full well did the old warrior know the unstable heart of the Israelites, and fearfully did he look into the mists of the future, lest they should forget God. But he had done his part. Under the blessing of Jehovah he had led this vast multitude across the Jordan, defeated many great kings, taken proud cities, and divided the land among the Israelites. So Joshua, that great soldier, died with the name of God upon his lips.

How Israel Forgot Its Past

FOR a few years after the death of Joshua, the people were brave, active and God-fearing. Those who remembered Joshua kept his faith alive. But as the old men died, the younger people thought it troublesome to be always on the watch for enemies, and they gave themselves more and more to the making of wealth. They were very happy, and they lived very cheerfully, and their wives sang the old songs, and the children grew up among the vineyards and in the cities with all the comforts and delights of a powerful nation.

So it came about that when really wicked nations threatened them with war, the Israelites, instead of destroying them, made friends with their enemies for the sake of peace. The result was that they caught the infection of wickedness from their enemies, and instead of remaining a peculiar people—that is to say, the one nation on the earth who worshiped One Invisible God, and lived in cleanliness and righteousness—they became like the heathen, committing the same sins and worshiping images.

But always there remained among the Israelites a sacred few who remembered God and obeyed His commandments.

Deborah, the Noble Woman
Who Saved Her People from Their Enemy

Such was Deborah, wife of Lapidoth. Deborah loved her people, and even fought with them against their enemies. It was this noble woman who roused Israel to remembrance of God, when the Canaanites, under Sisera, came against them with a vast army. She sent the Israelite Barak, and bade him summon an army to destroy Sisera. Barak said he would not fight unless Deborah herself went with him, for she was held almost sacred by the now craven and

113

Camels and burros carrying great loads plod the dusty roads of the Holy Land, winding through hills and plains familiar in Bible days.

repentant Israelites. So Deborah went with Barak, and Sisera's army was destroyed. Once more peace came to the land, but once again Israel relapsed into ease and carelessness and idolatry.

Then there came against the Israelites certain Arabian tribes, the Midianites, who made tremendous havoc in the land, destroying all the cornfields and vineyards, sheep, oxen and asses, and reducing Israel to the extremest horrors of poverty and want.

Gideon Sends Home 22,000 Cowards and Keeps 300 Heroes

In this awful hour of national peril, Gideon arose as deliverer. Guided by God, he sent to all the tribes of Israel for warriors to fight against the mighty host of Midian, and 32,000 men flocked to him. But Gideon would not have so large an army, lest they should say, "By our own arm we got the victory." So Gideon declared that any man who feared should return home, and 22,000 cowards forsook the host of Israel. But even 10,000 was too great a number; Gideon kept only 300. When night was come, he gave to each of his 300 a horn, and a torch in an earthen pitcher. He led them down from the mountain where they had encamped, to the plain in which the host of Midian, seeming as numerous as the sand on the seashore, lay sleeping by their fires.

At a signal from Gideon, the Israelites crashed together 300 pitchers, flashed into the air 300 torches, and blew with a loud blast 300 horns. The host of Midian started from their sleep to hear a frightful war shout in their ears, and to see torches advancing against them on every side. Stricken by panic, they grasped their weapons, and, in the confusion of darkness, smote one against the other, and fled, beaten and discomfited, before the Israelites.

Yet again Israel sank into idolatry, and when Gideon was dead one of his sons, Abimelech, made himself a king, and brought evil on the land. Then came the Philistines on one side, and the Ammonites on the other, and the news spread through Israel of the most terrible ravages.

Gideon led them

Jephthah, an outlaw, was chosen as deliverer, and he saved Israel. But there is a sad incident in this strange outlaw's victory. Touched by the mercy of God in choosing him, a poor outlaw, to take up the sword of Joshua and Barak and Gideon, he vowed before the battle that if victory was his he would sacrifice to Jehovah whatsoever his eyes first beheld coming out of his house to welcome him. And it came to pass after the battle that as he returned to his home his little daughter first ran out to greet him; and she was his only child. And Jephthah was utterly cast down, and told the child his vow. But she persuaded him to keep it, asking him to grant her two months to mourn alone in the mountain. At the end of that time the little maid returned to her father, who sacrificed her according to his vow. And thereafter it was a custom in the land "that the daughters of Israel went yearly to lament the daughter of Jephthah the Gileadite four days in a year."

Poor Jephthah's life was greatly troubled to its end. For some of the Israelites, jealous of his power, rose up against him, and there was a long and troublesome tribal war, which disturbed all the country. But Jephthah conquered again and again, and after his death there was peace for some years, the judges ruling the land till the coming of the mighty Samson, at the hour when the Philistines were plaguing Israel on every side.

116

Samson the Strong Man

THERE were a husband and wife among the Israelites who lived on a hill named Zorah, from which they could see the country known as Philistia. They had no children, and the wife would often sit at the door looking across the valley of Philistia, wishing that she had a son. Very beautiful, but very bitter for an Israelite, was the view of this hill. For there dwelt a people who worshiped idols, lived evil lives, and mocked, harried and murdered the Israelites.

"Oh, if I had a son," the poor Israelite woman must often have thought, as she looked across the valley, "he might grow up and deliver us from these Philistines!"

One day a vision came to her, and she knew that a son was to be born to her, and that this son should grow up in strength such as no man had known before, and that with his right arm he should begin the great work of rescuing Israel from the oppression of the Philistines. This child was to be devoted by her to the service of God; his hair was never to be cut; he was to be kept from wine and all drink that impairs the health of the body; and he was to be specially marked out for serving Israel's God, the great Jehovah.

The child was born, and received the name Samson. Gladly did the father and mother watch the growth of this boy, and with different eyes now did they look upon the valley beneath them, where the Philistines worshiped the idol Dagon.

"Ah," thought they, "the Philistines rejoice now, and are puffed up with pride; but every day that sees the limbs of our son enlarge, and the strength of his body increase, brings these Philistines nearer to the hour of their doom." And they educated Samson as the vision had told.

When he was grown to man's estate, and his strength was such that nothing could stand against him, instead of expressing hatred for the Philistines, he seemed to be well disposed toward them, and actually bade his father make arrangements for him to marry a Philistine woman. The parents were horrified and shocked, but they dared not stand against the will of their terrible son. They had obeyed the commands of the vision, but they had not taught the boy to be lord of his will.

He seized its jaws in his hands

On his way to visit this woman, a young lion sprang out at Samson. He was unarmed, but, waiting for the savage beast, he seized its two open jaws in his hand as it leapt towards him, and with a great jerk of his wrists tore it in two like a sheet of parchment. On his second visit, he found that bees had hived honey in the carcass of the lion, and he took of the honey and ate it.

At the marriage festival he was surrounded by merry people, and to thirty of these Philistine men he put a riddle, vowing that he would give thirty changes of raiment to any who could guess it. This was Samson's riddle: "Out of the eater came forth meat, and out of the strong came forth sweetness." The men could not answer it, but they came secretly to Samson's wife, and threatened that if she did not entice the answer out of Samson they would burn her house down. So she teased Samson till he told her of the lion and the honey, and she instructed the Philistines how they should answer. When they guessed the riddle, Samson saw how it had come to pass, and he was angered. But they had answered, and he had to give them the raiment. So he went in his wrath and slew thirty men, and got the raiment and brought it to those who had answered his riddle. Very angry, he sent his wife away and she returned to her father. Samson went back to his own home.

The Terrible Revenge Against the Philistines

With time, his anger cleared away, and he thought with kindness of the wife he had deserted. He killed and prepared a kid, and went down to the place where she lived, intending to be friends with her again; but he found that her father had married her to another man. Wild with rage, this giant caught three hundred foxes, tied them tail to tail, with a lighted firebrand knotted between the two tails, and turned them into the cornfields and vineyards of the Philistines. So great was the damage done by this fire that when the Philistines heard who had done it, and why, they went to the house of Samson's wife and burned her and her father.

Samson was more angered than ever, and, plunging in among the Philistines, he slew many of them in his fury, and, like a madman, dashed out the brains of all who came in his way. Afterward, sullen and full of sorrow, he retired to the top of a mountain and brooded over his unhappiness, still forgetting God.

Now the Philistines perceived that in this Israelite they had a mighty enemy, who must be subdued at all costs. Great was his strength, and terrible was the fear he inspired; but one man could not stand against a nation, and so they pursued him to the mountain. Here they met Israelites who were cowards, who lived willingly under the Philistine rule, and these men, hoping to make friends with their oppressors, offered to deliver Samson into their hands.

How Samson Was Caught and Bound

They scaled the rock and rebuked Samson for stirring up the Philistines. To their surprise, he allowed them to bind him and lead him down in triumph to the Philistines at the foot of the hill. When they saw the giant bound, they shouted with joy—for they feared this one man more than an army of Israelites. But as he reached them Samson stretched his great muscles. The cords burst like flax, and he stood out free and terrible. Smitten with panic at the sight of the free giant, the Philistines turned and fled, and Samson, seizing the jawbone of an ass, plunged into the midst of them, and slew them.

Then Samson went to a strong city called Gaza, and when it was night the people lay in wait for him at the gate, meaning to fall suddenly upon him in the morning and slay him. But Samson rose at midnight—very still and silent was the sleeping city—and, going to the gate where the assassins lay with their weapons, he plucked up the posts, the bars and the gate of the strong city, and carried them on his back to the top of a hill.

Samson, blind and powerless

Gaza, mentioned in Genesis 10:19, has always been a busy caravan city on the ancient commercial highway along the Mediterranean between Egypt and the Holy Land. Here, Samson carried away a city gate, and later destroyed a temple upon himself.

Samson Betrayed by Delilah

By this time the fear of Samson's name was greatly increased, and the Philistines trembled at the sound of it.

But Samson, marked out for great and noble things, became a victim to the spell of a wicked person. He gave himself up to a woman, Delilah, and forgot, while he amused himself in her company, the great destiny which had been marked out for him from his birth. Then the crafty Philistines saw their opportunity.

They came to Delilah and bribed her to wile out of Samson the secret of his vast strength. Samson put her off for a long time, but she pretended to be angry with him, and said that it proved he did not love her that he would not tell her this secret. Then Samson, weak in this woman's hands, told his secret; that his hair had never been cut from the day of his birth, that if ever it was shaven he would become weak and like other men. Then, while he slept, she cut the hair from his head, and he woke up without power, and the Philistines sprang upon him. They bored out his eyes, bound him with fetters of brass, and put him in the prison house at Gaza to grind corn. This man, who might have delivered Israel from the heathen, ground corn in a prison house like a harnessed ox, blind and powerless.

A Little Lad Leads Samson to the Great Feast

Such a victory was ascribed by these heathen Philistines to their god Dagon, and they immediately prepared a great feast in his honor. The mighty lords and the fine ladies of Philistia rejoiced at this festival, and wild grew their merriment. They drank much wine and danced round their idol, singing and rioting. Some said: "Call for Samson, that he may make us sport!" This was the great jest of the festival—Samson should be brought to them to make sport for them.

123

Israel's hero, Samson, was born in the town of Zorah, atop a hill across the Valley of Sorek. Here also lived Delilah, who betrayed Samson to his enemies, the Philistines. They captured him after his long hair had been cut, and "bound him with fetters of brass" (Judges 16:4-21) to carry him to their capital, Gaza.

Think of the picture. The prison door opens; a little lad comes out, leading by the hand an immense man whose shoulders are bowed as though with shame, whose head is bent as though to hide the horror of his eyeless sockets. He is bound; he is harmless. A shout goes up to the skies: "Behold the man we once feared! Look at the terror which affrighted us! Blind! Weak! Led by a little lad! This is Samson, the mighty Samson!"

Perhaps Delilah was among those who laughed at the prisoner.

Samson was teased, and driven to and fro to make sport for the Philistines, even as in Spain to this day they bait a bull till it is maddened. Thousands of people looked on and laughed from the roof of a vast building—laughed in derision of Samson.

And Samson grew weary.

"Let us rest a little," he said to the boy, who led him to and fro. Think of these words addressed by the once mighty man to the boy: "Suffer me that I may feel the pillars whereupon the house standeth, that I may lean upon them." In mercy, the boy guided his prisoner to the pillars of the great house, and Samson, panting and spent, rested there, with his arms laid against them, his head bowed.

The revelry went on. In a minute or two the giant would be back again making sport for them. The wine went round. The music continued. Flowers were tossed about. The dancers swung in the sun. The statue of Dagon rose in the midst of it.

And as Samson heard the songs and the sound of the music, and the taunts of the Philistines, there swept over his soul the memory of what he had once been. His hands gripped together, and a sob rose in his throat. God had intended him to save his people from the oppression of these heathen; and, instead, he had lived like the heathen themselves. Oh, bitter thought!

Samson Dies with the Philistines

He might have been a Moses, a Joshua, the hero of a nation; but his name would become a proverb of shame to all nations. He was shamed. The memory of his mother rose in his heart. The days of his childhood returned, sweet and beautiful. Once, once he had been pure. Once he had been devoted to God! His arms tightened round the pillar; the sob broke in his throat. He remembered God, and called to Him; "Strengthen me, I pray Thee, only this once." The music waxed louder, the revelry more riotous. The cries increased for Samson! Samson! Samson! The giant bowed himself with all his might upon the pillars, and saying, "Let me die with the Philistines!" he brought the house down with a roar like thunder, and perished in the midst of his enemies.

The Story of Ruth and Naomi

WE now pause in the troubled story of Israel, and for a little while listen to a romantic history which shows us something of the sweetness, gentleness, and kindness of those distant times. At this time there was peace throughout the land; but there was also a great famine.

Elimelech, with his wife Naomi, and his two sons Mahlon and Chilion, made a journey from their house to the foreign and heathen country of Moab, because of the famine. They found land and food in this strange country, and were hospitably received. Elimelech and the two sons were perfectly content with it; but Naomi sighed often for her homeland and for the company of her kinspeople.

Elimelech died, and his two sons married Moabite women. They felt themselves now thoroughly settled in the new land, and must have smiled to hear their mother Naomi constantly sighing for the land of Judah. But presently the two sons died, and poor Naomi was left alone in this foreign country, with no one to care for her but these two foreign women who had married her sons. More than ever she longed to return.

When it came to her ears that prosperity had returned to the land of Judah, the widow said that she would return to her own people. Her daughters-in-law said they would go with her, but she bade them return each to her mother's house. The two women wept, and one of them returned to her mother's house. But Ruth, the other daughter-in-law, clave to Naomi.

"Behold," said Naomi, "thy sister-in-law is gone back unto her people, and unto her gods: return thou after thy sister-in-law." But Ruth still clave to her, and said:

> *Entreat me not to leave thee, or to return*
> *from following after thee;*
> *For whither thou goest, I will go;*
> *And where thou lodgest, I will lodge;*
> *Thy people shall be my people,*
> *And thy God my God;*
> *Where thou diest, will I die, and there will*
> *I be buried;*
> *The Lord do so to me, and more also, if*
> *aught but death part thee and me.*

Then Naomi loved her daughter-in-law, and the two women journeyed on together, growing in love as the miles passed behind them.

When they reached Naomi's country—the country of Israel—it was the time of barley harvest. Ruth, therefore, in order that she might get food for her mother-in-law, went to glean corn in the fields of a rich man, a relative of Naomi's dead husband.

This rich man, whose name was Boaz, saw the lovely foreign woman among the reapers, and inquired who she might be. He learned that this beautiful woman had come a long journey with her mother-in-law, even into a foreign country, and that for love of this poor mother-in-law she now gleaned among the corn to earn

Reapers in the Field of Boaz, near Bethlehem, gathering ripened grain in the same manner as did Ruth. (Ruth 2:3)

Edward Laning

MOSES BREAKETH THE TABLES

The twentieth century American artist, Edward Laning, is known for his
murals showing figures of exuberant vitality. Moses is coming down from
Sinai and finds the Israelites worshipping a golden calf. "Moses' anger
waxed hot, and he cast the tables out of his hands" (Exodus 32:19).

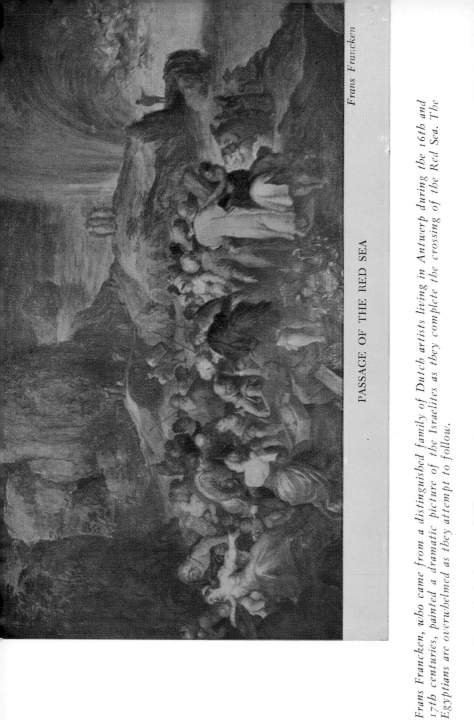

Frans Francken

PASSAGE OF THE RED SEA

Frans Francken, who came from a distinguished family of Dutch artists living in Antwerp during the 16th and 17th centuries, painted a dramatic picture of the Israelites as they complete the crossing of the Red Sea. The Egyptians are overwhelmed as they attempt to follow.

"For whither thou goest, I will go"

ood and lodging. The rich and prosperous Boaz looked upon
Ruth as he heard this story, and, seeing her toil there so patiently
and meekly, his heart was moved with a great admiration.

So Boaz loved Ruth the Moabitess, and he made her his wife.
And when a son was born to them, whose name was Obed, Naomi
became nurse to it, and the family lived together in great peace and
contentment. Thus was Ruth rewarded for her faithful love for
her mother-in-law, and in the peace of her simple days in Israel she
ound joy.

But how great would her happiness have been if she had known
how the child whose play she loved to watch was one day to become the father of Jesse, who was to become the father of the great
David, through whom was to come Jesus Christ, the Light of the
World and the Saviour of Mankind.

Camels, almost completely hidden by their cargoes of wheat, carry heavy loads of the golden grain to the nearest stone-paved threshing floor, where kernels of wheat will be released by threshing-boards.

Samuel and the Great Change

IN THE days of Samson, the high priest of Israel was a man named Eli, who sat upon the great throne in the gateway of the Tabernacle, meditating on the mysteries of God and man, and watching the people as they came to worship on the feast days. It chanced one day that this old man on his seat took offense at a woman kneeling in prayer before the sanctuary, imagining from the earnestness with which she prayed that she had come straight from the riot and revelry of the holiday festivities. He spoke harshly to her, and the woman, whose name was Hannah, lifted up her face and told him the real truth. She prayed thus earnestly because, more than anything else in the world, she desired a son. The old priest, touched by her sincerity, and ashamed of his own suspicions, bade her to be comforted, for God would surely answer a prayer so earnest and pure.

Hannah vowed that if indeed her prayer were answered she would give her son to the service of God. A son was born to her, and she "called his name Samuel, saying, Because I have asked him of the Lord." The good woman remembered her vow; and as soon as she was able she brought the infant to the old priest, and gave him up to the service of the Tabernacle. While the little lad Samuel grew up in the solemn atmosphere of this place of worship, the sons of Eli lived outside in the world, in selfishness and evil-doing. The people hated these young men, and scorned them as the sons of the High Priest, who surely should have been better than themselves; but Eli rebuked them not, and restrained them not.

One night, as the old priest lay in bed, the child Samuel came to his side, and asked if Eli had called him. Eli, between waking and slumber, looked with surprise at the little boy. No, he told him, he had not called, let Samuel go back to bed. A second time Samuel came, for distinctly he had heard a voice call him by name; but again Eli sent him back. Then a third time the same thing happened; and now the old priest, roused to perceive that some mystery was in the night, bade the boy return to his couch, and when the voice called him again, to reply, "Speak, Lord, for Thy servant heareth."

The mysterious message that Samuel heard in the gray light of dawn was dreadful, and he hid it from the old priest. The voice had declared that the sons of Eli were to die, that ruin was to overtake his family, and that the old man was to be left desolate upon the earth. Eli commanded the child to tell him what he had heard; and when at last Samuel did so, the poor old priest bowed his head and sighed, "It is the Lord. Let Him do what seemeth Him good."

They destroyed their idols

Times of horror occurred. Enemies of Israel arose on all sides. The sons of Eli were slain in a general rout, the Ark was captured; and Eli, hearing the terrible news, fell dead.

It was in this long time of ruin and devastation that Samuel grew from childhood to youth, and from youth to manhood.

Through the distress and apparent ruin of Israel, he lived in communion with God; and the heartbroken nation began slowly to reverence him, and to hope that he might prove their deliverer.

One day he declared his message to the people. They must give up worshiping idols. They must turn to the Invisible God of Righteousness. Only thus could they escape destruction. The bracing message of the prophet had its effect. Israel listened, awoke from the stupor of idolatry, and, destroying their miserable images and idols, went up against their enemies like a nation of men, and in the strength of God's righteousness destroyed their enemies.

It was the one great victory obtained by Israel under Samuel. Peace followed for a time, but later, the people, seeing their enemies growing strong once more, came to the prophet and made a strange request. They asked him to give them a king.

Such a request was terrible to the old prophet. A king over Israel! Was it not Israel's pride that they had for King the Invisible and Eternal God of Righteousness? Was it not their scorn that heathen people bowed before an earthly ruler? Was God to be displaced?

The Israelites persisted in their demand. They wanted to be like other people. All the nations had a king; they, too, would have a king. Thus came to pass one of the greatest national changes ever made in the history of the world. Alone among all the nations on earth, the Israelites had adored as their King an invisible Power, whom they called "The Eternal." They felt that the earth had been made by some Power who was eternal. Because this One Eternal Power was the greatest, they worshiped it. But now a change was to be made; the Israelites were to become as other people. They clamored for a visible king who would lead them into battle against their enemies. In making this tremendous change, the nation of

Israel lost the greatest of its glories.

Some time after the Israelites had made their request of the prophet, Samuel was on a journey and came across two wayfaring men. One of them was of great stature, and very handsome to look upon; his name was Saul, and he was in search of his father's asses, which had strayed. The other man was this Saul's servant. "Now the Lord had told Samuel a day before Saul came, saying, 'Tomorrow about this time I will send thee a man out of the land of Benjamin, and thou shalt anoint him to be captain over my people Israel.'" Samuel felt, as he looked upon Saul, that this was the man chosen by God to be the king demanded by Israel. He spoke to Saul, and persuaded the young man to spend the night with him. On the morrow he went a little way with Saul, and then, taking a

vial of oil, poured the contents upon Saul's head as a sign that he was "anointed" to be king.

Samuel went back and told the people of Israel how God had chosen Saul. Before a great assembly of the people, he brought Saul forward, and said, " 'See ye whom the Lord hath chosen, that there is none like him among all the people?' And all the people shouted and said, 'God save the king.' " Samuel then reminded the nation of their duty to God, and counseled them to follow righteousness.

A war broke out, and Saul, who was still working in the fields, called Israel to arms. The battle ended in a victory for Israel, and Saul became the hero of the nation. Then did the old Samuel feel that he might relinquish the government, and he called the people

The enemy advanced in a whirlwind of fury

together and uttered his farewell. "Behold, here I am; witness against me before the Lord, and before His anointed. Whose ox have I taken, or whose ass have I taken, or whom have I defrauded? Whom have I oppressed, or of whose hand have I received any bribe to blind mine eyes therewith?"

Then, to the Eternal God Samuel ascribed the justice of his rule, and he counseled Israel to fear the Eternal Power and serve Him in truth.

So Saul became king of Israel, and the prophet retired from his labors.

The First King of Israel

SAUL was a man of immense height, of singular beauty. And he loved his country deeply. But he was also subject to moods of such terrible gloom that occasionally they carried him to the verge of madness. At one moment he was a happy warrior, at the next a sullen, melancholy victim of a dreadful mania.

His reign was one of almost constant warfare. The first great struggle, after Samuel's retirement, was with the Philistines.

Saul had been carefully preparing for battle with these mighty people, when his high-spirited son, the dashing, light-hearted Jonathan, impulsively attacked a garrison of the Philistines and brought the whole nation about Saul's ears.

The enemy advanced with thirty thousand chariots, six thousand horsemen, and so many foot-soldiers that they were like the sands of the seashore in number. Israel was blown like dust before the whirlwind of their fury. The people hid in caves and thickets, on mountain tops, and in the depths of pits—anywhere to escape the vengeance of the advancing Philistines.

Even Saul fled. It looked as if a final and crushing blow had

The village of Ashdod (today called
Isdud), where the Philistines took the
Ark after capturing it from the Israelites.
(I Sam. 5:1)

fallen upon the Hebrews. The Philistines swept, undisputed, over the country.

But Saul, with a small force of loyal warriors, determined to make one stroke for freedom. He sent for Samuel to come and offer sacrifices to the Lord, to pray for victory over their enemies.

The days passed, and Samuel did not come. The impatient King then took the sacred office on himself, and did what only the high priest should have done. Samuel arrived finally, and condemned Saul for his act, telling him that, for this sin, the crown was to go out of Saul's family. Another than Jonathan his son should sit upon the throne of Israel.

Jonathan, knowing nothing of what had taken place, was impatient at his father's delay. One day, with only his armor-bearer at his side, he stole upon a host of Philistines, and slew twenty of them. The enemy were in confusion over his swift attack, and fled for their lives in disorder.

Saul's watchers saw the flight, and in a moment Saul was at the head of his little band pursuing the fleeing Philistines. He reorganized his army, and victory was his. Wherever he went, the foes of Israel scattered like chaff in the terrible wind of his sword. From being a weak and enfeebled people, Israel had now become a nation of warriors, and Saul's name rang like a war cry through all the regions of the earth.

After this victory over the Philistines, Samuel came to the King and declared it to be the will of Heaven that Saul should destroy the Amalekites. The war was to be one of punishment. Saul was not to seek territory or gold. He was to destroy utterly a wicked and abominable people. This punishment was to teach a lesson to all nations. Nothing was to be left of the Amalekites, because they had sinned themselves out of humanity, and were abhorrent to God. Even the best of their sheep and oxen had to be slain, because the whole nation and everything they owned were evil. All was to be destroyed.

So Saul smote Amalek, but Saul drove before him, as wages of battle, the flocks and herds of the horrible people. Samuel, discovering his disobedience, said to him, "Because thou has rejected the word of the Lord, He hath also rejected thee from being king."

Saul was terrified, and begged Samuel, "I pray thee pardon my sin." But Samuel refused, repeating that because Saul had not obeyed the word of the Lord, God would not let him be king over Israel any longer.

Saul fell into despair and melancholy. During one of the fits of insanity which came upon him, a shepherd boy from Bethlehem was brought to him. The name of this boy was David, and he played upon the harp so sweetly that he soothed the King, and Saul made him his minstrel and armor-bearer.

A strange thing had happened. The boy who gave peace to the troubled King was a boy whom Samuel, at the command of God, had secretly anointed to be king of Israel. More, he was to become so great a poet that his poems—to be known as the Psalms of David—were to give comfort to the sorrowful and courage to the faint of heart in every nation under the sun.

But in these days David knew only that he had been called from tending his father's sheep, to see the wonderful old prophet of Israel, Samuel, and that this venerable hero of the nation had poured oil upon David's head and anointed him the servant of God.

Guessing nothing of his great future, the boy, having given peace to the warrior-king of Israel, returned to his sheep. But when it was told to him that a mighty giant of the Philistines, Goliath, had challenged any man of Israel to fight with him, and that even Saul had held back, David left his flocks again and came down to do battle for Israel.

Saul tried to dissuade him, but David told him that God would deliver him from the mighty Philistine. Then Saul said, "Go, and the Lord be with thee." And he put on David a helmet of brass, and a coat of mail, and gave him a sword to go up against Goliath.

The young shepherd boy was not used to weapons like these,

The hill in the background covers the ruins of Gath, claimed to be the home of the giant, Goliath. Today it is called Tell-es-Safi. (I Sam. 17:4)

From the dry gorge of this brook in the Valley of Elah, young David chose five smooth stones for his sling (I Samuel 17:40), which he later used to slay the giant Philistine, Goliath.

and he refused them. "And he took his staff in his hand, and chose him five smooth stones out of the brook, and put them in a shepherd's bag which he had . . . and his sling was in his hand: and he drew near to the Philistine."

With rage and astonishment, the huge Goliath saw advancing toward him, not an armed warrior, but a handsome, dark-haired lad with bright eyes, who wore simple rustic clothes, and carried in his hand only a sling for casting stones. The giant cursed the boy, and told him his flesh should surely feed the fowls. David took a stone from his bag and fitted it into his sling.

With unerring aim he sent the stone flying, and it struck Goliath on the forehead, and brought him stumbling and stunned to the earth. Then David leaped upon the prostrate giant, and with Goliath's own sword hewed off his head.

This was the beginning of David's fame. He now became a warrior of Israel, and he and Jonathan, the King's son, were like brothers. But the troubled spirit of the King began to suspect David and to be jealous of him. The people praised David; and the King heard it, and was bitter.

Saul decided to kill David, who was forced to escape into the mountains. Full of rage and madness, the King massacred everybody who showed the smallest kindness to the poor, harried outlaw. Twice David had Saul in his power, and could have killed him; but—loving the unhappy, demented King—he offered him no hurt.

It was at this time that the Philistines once more rose in force, determined to destroy Israel. This diverted Saul's thoughts from David, and in his fear he sought out a witch at Endor, and asked her to call up before him the ghost of Samuel.

Now Samuel had been dead some time, but the witch, who deceived people by pretending that ghosts appeared at her bidding, called upon the prophet to appear. To her amazement and terror, there actually arose the vision of a real ghost, Samuel's spirit from the other world.

David fitted a stone into his sling

The old prophet of Israel, covered with a mantle, stood before her, and solemnly declared that on the morrow Saul and his sons would be with him in the land of the dead.

This prophecy came true. On the very next day the Philistines routed Israel at Mount Gilboa. Jonathan was killed in battle, and Saul, bleeding from his wounds and broken in spirit, fell upon his own sword and destroyed himself. David, when he heard of this desolation, did not rejoice that his oppressor was dead, but uttered one of the most beautiful lamentations in history:

> The beauty of Israel is slain upon thy high places; how are the mighty fallen!
>
> Tell it not in Gath, publish it not in the streets of Askelon;
>
> Lest the daughters of the Philistines rejoice, lest the daughters of the uncircumcised triumph.
>
> Ye mountains of Gilboa, let there be no dew, neither let there be rain, upon you, nor fields of offerings.
>
> For there the shield of the mighty is vilely cast away, the shield of Saul, as though he had not been anointed with oil.
>
> From the blood of the slain, from the fat of the mighty, the bow of Jonathan turned not back, and the sword of Saul returned not empty.
>
> Saul and Jonathan were lovely and pleasant in their lives, and in their deaths they were not divided:
>
> They were swifter than eagles, they were stronger than lions.
>
> Ye daughters of Israel, weep over Saul, who clothed you in scarlet, with other delights, who put on ornaments of gold upon your apparel.
>
> How are the mighty fallen in the midst of the battle! O Jonathan, thou wast slain in thine high places.
>
> I am distressed for thee, my brother Jonathan: very pleasant hast thou been unto me: thy love to me was wonderful, passing the love of women.
>
> How are the mighty fallen, and the weapons of war perished!

Thus perished Israel's first king, and with him died the young prince Jonathan before the crown of Israel had descended upon him.

David, the Shepherd King

David tended flocks

THE shepherd who had been fetched from tending his father's flocks, that the mighty prophet might look upon him, who had comforted the warrior Saul by his singing, who had slain the Philistine giant with a sling, and who had become the bosom friend of the King's son, was now himself king.

Travellers, their faces shielded from the hot sun by the typical Arab *kefiyeh* veil, move along a dusty road outside Jerusalem.

The poor man had but one lamb

How David Rose by Hard Fighting
to Be King Over All Israel

At first his right to reign was disputed by the heirs of King Saul.
David had to fight for his crown. The struggle was hard and
fierce: but in the end he subdued those who contested his claim. In
a brief time he was king over all Israel, had conquered the strong
city of Jerusalem, and made it the capital of his kingdom.

His first idea, when he had made Jerusalem the city of the king, was a poetical idea. He sent for the Ark—that sacred symbol of God's blessing on Israel—and housed it in the capital city. Then he rejoiced, and made a poem to the glory of God.

Sing unto the Lord, all the earth; show forth from day to day His salvation. Declare His glory among the heathen; His marvelous works among all nations. For great is the Lord, and greatly to be praised; He is also to be feared above all gods. For all the gods of the people are idols; but the Lord made the heavens.

He pointed to the hills, to the ocean, to the forest, to the flowers, to the green pastures; he looked up to the moon riding in the star-lit heaven; he listened to the race of the wind and the leaping roar. of the thunder.

"His judgments," said David, "are in all the earth." God, for him, was the Power Who had made all things, and without Whom nothing was made that is made. Man was the creature of this Creator. Only by studying the works of God, his Maker, could man be happy and glad.

And yet there were moments when evil ideas visited David's brain, and he was swept into cruel and degrading actions.

The Sad Story of David's Evil

Looking one day from his palace, he saw a woman whose face so pleased him that he desired to make her his wife. He sent for her, and discovered that she was Bathsheba, the wife of a Hittite, Uriah. In order that he might marry her, he sent Uriah to Joab, the commander of his forces, and secretly told Joab to place Uriah in so prominent a place in the next battle that he would certainly be killed. This wicked command was acted upon, and Uriah fell dead before the enemies of the King.

149

How Nathan Rebuked David

David then married Bathsheba; and one day afterward there came to him a prophet named Nathan, who related a story to him:

"There were two men in one city; the one rich, and the other poor. The rich man had exceeding many flocks and herds; but the poor man had nothing, save one little ewe lamb, which he had brought up and nourished; and it grew up together with him, and with his children; it did eat of his own meat, and drank of his own cup, and lay in his bosom, and was unto him as a daughter. And there came a traveler unto the rich man, and he spared to take of his own flock, and of his own herd, to dress for the wayfaring man that was come unto him; but took the poor man's lamb, and dressed it for the man that was come to him."

David started up with burning indignation:

"As God liveth," he cried, "the man that hath done this thing shall surely die."

The Repentance and Punishment of King David

Then did the prophet, looking upon the King, utter the great judgment:

"Thou art the man."

David saw what was meant, and as the stern prophet pronounced the displeasure of God at an action so base and cruel, he realized the horror of his crime.

"I have sinned against the Lord," he exclaimed.

"The Lord also hath put away thy sin," answered the prophet.

The fact of David's confession and repentance—because it was sincere repentance—brought him at once the forgiveness of God. His transgressions were removed from him. While he sinned he was under the judgment of God; as soon as he repented he was restored to God's favor.

150

But punishment had to fall upon him. The child which was born to Bathsheba and David sickened and pined. David fasted, and lay prone upon the earth in an agony. The father in his heart cried unto God. The son was dear to him; he besought God to have mercy and let the little one live.

But the child died. Then at last David rose, bathed himself, put on fresh clothing, and sat down to eat.

"What thing is this that thou hast done?" asked the people about him.

"Thou didst fast and weep for the child, while it was alive; but when the child was dead, thou didst rise and eat bread."

And David said; "While the child was yet alive, I fasted and wept; for I said, who can tell whether God will be gracious to me, that the child may live? But now he is dead, wherefore should I fast? Can I bring him back again? I shall go to him, but he shall not return to me."

From this time forward the life of David was one of incessant struggle with sorrow, trouble and misfortune.

David Mourns Absalom, His Son

His favorite son, Absalom, raised a rebellion against David, and actually sought to destroy his own father that he himself might become the king. David reluctantly allowed his troops to dispute the progress of Absalom's army, but bade the commander deal gently with the young man. In this battle David's army obtained the victory, and Absalom, fleeing for his life on a mule, was caught in the bough of an oak tree by his head. The mule went on, leaving him hanging from the tree, helpless, until Joab killed him by thrusting three darts through his heart.

When the messenger of Joab reached David, the King was sitting between the two gates of the city.

"Tidings, my lord the king!" cried the messenger; "for the Lord

151

The tomb of King David's son, Absolom, in the Kidron Valley, Jerusalem. (II Sam. 18:17)

hath avenged thee this day of all them that rose up against thee."

David asked, "Is the young man Absalom safe?" And when he heard that Absalom was dead, he went up into the chamber over the gate, and cried out, "O my son Absalom, my son, my son Absalom! Would God I had died for thee, O Absalom, my son, my son!"

And now came war among the tribes of Israel; and as David's life drew to its close, peace seemed to have fled from the earth. He saw his land afflicted by the scourges of the sword and of disease. Evil befell Israel, and God appeared to veil His face. But David besought God to have mercy, and continued faithful in his worship. When he was an old man, another son of his named Adonijah rose up against him, and proclaimed himself to be the king of Israel. But David declared that Solomon, Bathsheba's son, should be king of Israel, and Solomon was anointed. Adonijah returned, after this, and made peace with his brother.

The last act of David was to assemble all the people together, and to declare that his great wish had been to build a mighty temple to the honor and glory of the Lord, but that, because he had been a man of war and not of peace, God had suffered him not to accomplish his dream. Solomon, however, should see this temple rise from the earth, and to Solomon he gave the plans of the building, with all the costly materials he had amassed for its splendor.

David Goes Out into the Glory of a New Life

David, old and dying, spoke in his last breath of the glory of that Eternal God whose might, majesty and dominion had inspired all his songs. "Thine, O Lord, is the greatness, and the power, and the glory, and the victory, and the majesty; for all that is in the heaven and in the earth is Thine."

David is called "the man after God's own heart." That splendid title was earned by David because, though he fell many times, he always repented and sought help from God to be a nobler being.

King David's Tower in Jerusalem, overlooking the
road leading south toward Bethlehem.

King David's Tower, as it appears today.

The Reign of King Solomon

IT IS written in the Book of Chronicles that David "died in a good old age, full of days and riches, and Solomon his son reigned in his stead." At the beginning of his reign, Solomon had a strange dream. One night at Gibeon he seemed to hear the voice of God saying to him, "Ask what I shall give thee." The young King, who felt how difficult it was to govern a whole nation, asked not for glory, nor for riches, nor for a long life, but for wisdom. He was young, modest, anxious to do right. The Lord was pleased with Solomon for his unselfishness, and said to him, "Wisdom and knowledge is granted unto thee; and I will give thee riches, and wealth, and honor, such as none of the kings have had that have been before thee, and neither shall there any after thee have the like."

So every good thing was poured out upon Solomon, without his having asked for it.

Soon the whole kingdom was smiling and pleased over a decision of the King, which showed that, young as he was, he could read the hearts of those about him.

Two women were brought before him, with a baby which each claimed as her own. The real mother told the King that they both lived in the same house; each had had a child; but in her sleep, the other mother had rolled over on her baby, and it had died. Waking, and discovering what had happened, she wickedly took her dead child and put it in the other mother's bed, exchanging it for the living baby.

There was great excitement in the King's court. Both mothers talked loudly; one claiming this story was true, the other denying it. No one could actually prove which was telling the truth, and which a lie.

Solomon thought a while, and then commanded that a sword be brought and that the baby be divided and half given to each mother.

As he had known would happen, the real mother wept bitterly, begging the King to give the child, *alive,* to the other woman, but not to harm it. At once everyone understood that the child was hers, because she loved it so; and their admiration for their young King grew stronger.

Thus the popularity of Solomon spread among his people. And as he had applied himself to learning the wise proverbs of the ancients, he soon became renowned for his own wisdom.

For the first three years of his reign, Solomon worked to make

Then everyone knew that the child was hers

The Moslem mosque, of the Dome of the Rock, Jerusalem, built on the site of King Solomon's Temple.

A model of King Solomon's Temple, built in 1,000 B.C. It is claimed that the so-called "Wailing Wall' in the old section of Jerusalem is a part of the original Temple.

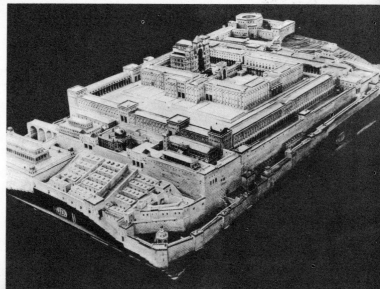

his kingdom great and safe against all enemies. He gathered about him thousands of chariots and horsemen, stationing them in the various chariot cities of the land and in Jerusalem. And for the chariots, he had horses brought from far-away Egypt. Riches came to him. It is said of him that he "made silver and gold at Jerusalem as plenteous as stones."   •

In addition to all this, Solomon set about the fulfillment of David's great and majestic dream, the building of the Temple. He sent far away for the most beautiful materials and the most skillful workmen; 30,000 Israelites were set to cut down the necessary timber: 80,000 slaves toiled in the quarries; 70,000 Israelites acted as porters. In the fourth year of his reign the foundation was laid, and in the eleventh this immense labor came to a close. The Temple was decorated with precious stones for beauty, and the building, the posts, the walls and the doors were all overlaid with gold.

Solomon was a born builder. He felt the poetry of beautiful forms, and dreamed in stone. Perhaps the building of the Temple fired him to attempt other mighty creations in wood and stone. He built a palace for himself which became one of the wonders of the world, and the story of its lordly pleasure grounds passed like a fairy tale into all languages. He built another palace for his wife, and a house supported entirely on pillars of sweet-smelling cedar wood.

Under the wise rule of Solomon the land of Israel prospered. A spirit of enthusiasm spread through the whole nation. The people gave themselves up to diligent labor, and their King made treaties with other countries. Very soon caravans were spreading far and wide in the East, carrying the merchandise of the Israelites. Travelers from other countries were moving with admiration among the streets of Jerusalem. It was difficult for the rich, prosperous and famous Israelite, going up to Solomon's gorgeous Temple, to remember that his ancestors had wailed under the lash of Pharaoh's taskmasters.

Such marvelous tales were told throughout all the East of

The Moslem mosque, Dome of the
Rock, in Jerusalem, stands on the site of
the sacred rock Moriah, where legend
says Isaac was laid by his father Abraham
as a sacrifice.

One of three ancient water reservoirs built by King Solomon in the 10th century, B.C. This pool lies about 2 miles west of the road from Jerusalem to Hebron, near its junction with the road to Bethlehem.

Solomon's magnificence and wisdom that the famous Queen of Sheba, a distant kingdom, determined to come and see for herself whether they could all be true.

She brought with her a mighty company of couriers, soldiers and attendants, and a train of camels carrying wonderful spices, great quantities of gold and precious stones.

She was amazed by what she beheld at the court of Solomon, and by the wisdom with which he answered her questions. Looking about her, she said to the King, "It is a true report which I heard in mine own land." And she gave him gifts of gold and jewels, and of spices more rare and delicious than any which had ever come into that country.

Such was the great glory of this wise and noble King. But as age crept upon him, the vision which he had seen so clearly in his youth dimmed before his eyes. He no longer felt the tremendous responsibility of being king; he no longer realized the need for wisdom; above all things, his reverence for God grew cold and faint. He was surrounded by every kind of pomp and magnificence; scarcely anything that he desired was impossible to him; and he grew gradually to consider himself not as the servant of the Lord, but only as the rich and powerful master of Israel.

His sin lay in this vanity, this appalling self-satisfaction of the rich man; it showed itself also in his yielding to the wishes of his wives to set up altars to strange gods.

Yet amidst all his wealth and magnificence he found no pleasure in life. "Vanity, vanity, all is vanity!" was the bitter cry of this envied King panoplied in splendor. He had had too much. Life could offer him nothing. He had ransacked the earth for his delight, and his soul cried out within him for something else.

Towards the end of his reign, which had begun with such modest reverence and had swelled into such bewildering magnificence, signs of a black tempest showed in the sky. Solomon, in search of wealth, power and magnificence, had laid heavy burdens on the people.

They were beginning to suffer more and more under his ex-

Arabs watching a procession in the Holy
Land, much as their ancestors might have
watched the great camel train of the
Queen of Sheba when she came to visit
King Solomon. (I Kings 10:1-13)

actions. Here and there could be heard murmured complaints and angry questionings. And then suddenly enemies appeared, stirring up revolt. War reared its head. Mutiny spread like a fire. To Jeroboam, an able man who had been advanced to a high post by Solomon himself, a prophet appeared, Ahijah of Shiloh, who rent his robe into twelve pieces, and, giving ten of them to Jeroboam, exclaimed: "Take these ten pieces; for thus saith the Lord, the God of Israel, Behold I will rend the kingdom out of the hand of Solomon, and will give ten tribes to thee." Solomon, hearing of this, for such news spread quickly, would have put Jeroboam to death. However, death was not for Jeroboam, but for Solomon himself. Jeroboam escaped safely to Egypt, and remained there until death came to Solomon, who, with his dying eyes, beheld not only the vanity of his life, but the ruin threatening his empire.

Thus ended the reign of Solomon, one of the wisest men of ancient times, and one of the most foolish.

Jerusalem prospered under Solomon's reign

Aged cypress trees guard the approach to
the ancient Moslem mosque in Jerusalem
known as the Dome of the Rock. Built
by Khalif Abd el-Melek in the seventh
century A.D., it stands on the location of
former Temples of Solomon and Herod.

The End of Glory

SOLOMON died nearly a thousand years before the birth of Christ, and the story of those thousand years is one of disaster and suffering. The death of Solomon closed a period in the story of Israel; the birth of Christ opened a period in the history of the whole world. The glory of this strange people is that, first of all nations, the Jews believed in one God; and from them came Jesus to be the Lord and Saviour of Mankind.

At first we see these people in the life of a single man, Abraham. He knew what so few people on the earth knew at that time—that there is one everlasting, invisible and perfect God. Because he had this saving faith, through him all the nations of the earth were to be blessed. He brought up his children in this faith. One of his descendants, Joseph, was sold into captivity, and in heathen Egypt became a powerful minister of the King. Famine overtook his brothers; he sent for them, and they emigrated to Egypt. In the course of time the descendants of these twelve brethren became so rich and powerful that the Egyptians hated them and feared them. The Jews were reduced to a state of slavery, and lived in the utmost misery for many years among their foreign tyrants.

Then a patriot arose among them, Moses, who led the twelve tribes out of Egypt, and conducted them into a country of their own, Canaan. They were a miserable nation at this time, broken by long years of slavery, and contaminated by the heathen superstitions of the Egyptians; they were almost incapable of rising to the grand idea of Abraham—that there is only one God, a God of Law, and that this one God is everlasting, invisible and perfect. But Moses gave them a wonderful code of laws, which helped them to be clean in their bodies and their habits, and braced their moral character.

167

Among them were young and brave men, and these, taking the sword, drove out their enemies before them, and established themselves in the promised land of Canaan. Prosperity came, and in their prosperity they grew luxurious and careless of the law. They found it a burden to think of a God Who is invisible, and they made for themselves idols, they married heathen women, and disobeyed the laws framed for their health. They grew weak and diseased, and their enemies came up against them and defeated them.

Then it occurred to them that all would be well if they had a king like other nations. Saul was anointed king over Israel, and he dispersed their enemies. The Israelites grew rich and prosperous again, and once again they forgot God. After Saul, David was king, and during his reign the kingdom became troubled by rebellion. David put down the rebellions, and made songs for the people, reminding them of the great and mighty things God had done for them in the past. He conceived the idea of building a glorious temple to the Creator of heaven and earth, giving the people something visible before their eyes which would remind them of the invisible God. But he died before he could carry out his plan.

Solomon, his son, succeeded him. The temple was built, but men were made slaves for the purpose, and as the beautiful structure rose to the glory of God, the builders bled, and groaned and died. Solomon built for his own satisfaction as an artist, not for the sake of Israel's religion. He lived for beautiful things, caring little for humanity, and he filled Jerusalem with pomp and splendor. While his country grew more powerful, his subjects groaned under the oppression of his tax-collectors, and at his death the kingdom was torn asunder.

Solomon was succeeded on the throne by his son Rehoboam. The nation, glad that Solomon the oppressor was dead, waited to see what the new King would do to lighten their burdens. While they waited, some of their more daring reformers sent for Jeroboam, Solomon's wise and skillful minister who had escaped into Egypt from the wrath of Solomon.

Jeroboam came out of Egypt, and at once put himself at the head of the gathering mutiny. He presented himself, with some of the chief people, before Rehoboam, and demanded reforms. Rehoboam asked time for consideration of the new ideas presented to him. He went to his old counselors first. They agreed that it would be wise for him to lighten the burdens of his subjects. Then he went to the young men, who argued that if he gave way to the people they would demand more and more from him till nothing was left of his kingship. Rehoboam thought that this was very clever advice. He put on a stern manner and told the reformers that "whereas my father did lade ye with a heavy yoke, I will add to your yoke: my father hath chastened you with whips, but I will chastise you with scorpions."

It is not easy to bully a whole nation. Rehoboam's bluster blew away before the wrath of Israel like the froth of waves in a northeast wind. Too late he discovered his folly. Revolution sprang up. Before he knew what had happened, he found himself ruling over only four of the tribes of Israel, while Jeroboam was king of the other eight.

The story of Israel is now the miserable story of a house divided against itself. The kingdom of Judah, reigned over by Rehoboam, was at ceaseless war with the kingdom of Israel, reigned over by Jeroboam. Foreign enemies came up against these warring factions, and misery and desolation spread through the fair land of Canaan. Both kings lived wicked lives. God was almost forgotten. Heathen practices and abominable vices took the place of spiritual worship and clean living. It seemed as if the divided house must fall; as if the promise made to Abraham must be broken; as if the whole people must perish.

Passing over the evil reigns of Rehoboam and Jeroboam, and over the reigns of their successors, we come to the story of a man who was not a king or a mighty captain, but whose history is one of the most remarkable in the world.

Elijah and King Ahab

Ravens brought food to him

JEZEBEL, the wife of Ahab, king of Israel, was a foreign princess. She came from the proud and rich country of Tyre, where people worshiped a god named Baal. The people of Tyre laughed at Israel's idea of a God, and the young Queen's haughty nature would not let her be satisfied with a few Tyrian worshipers of Baal at the court of her husband. She claimed that Baal should have equal rights with the God of Israel. If the God of Israel had temples, Baal must have temples too. If the God of Israel had

Elijah uttered a prophecy before the throne

priests and prophets, so must Baal. She could not allow her religion to be treated lightly. Ahab yielded to his Tyrian princess. Not only did he see the temple raised to Baal, and hundreds of the prophets of this false god feasting every day at the Queen's table, but he, the heir of David, allowed prophets of the true God to be driven away and persecuted as though they were wicked men. The sin of Ahab was that he thought one god was as good as another. He was flippant, tolerant, thoughtless.

One day there appeared at the King's palace a strange, stern man with flowing hair and bearded face. He was dressed in a robe made of camel's hair, with a leathern girdle about his loins. His presence created excitement at the luxurious court of the King—excitement and uneasiness. The courtiers were startled. Something in the old man's resolute gaze held them like a spell. Monarch and thinker looked into each other's eyes. The strange, stern man who had come from the loneliness of the wooded hills to the sumptuous palace of this easy-going King was Elijah the Tishbite, a man little known then, but the greatest man who had walked the earth since the days of Moses—a thinker.

In the loneliness of the hills, studying the wonders and the power of creation, this old, hard-thinking and silent man had come to feel the voice of God close to his soul. He knew that there was but one God, the invisible and eternal Power Who had made the heavens and the earth.

Elijah was not simply jealous of another nation's god, as was Jezebel. No; he saw the awful truth of the contrast—that while God demanded righteousness, Baal encouraged men and women to live like animals, without a conscience. Jezebel had set up a god in Israel who taught men and women to be beast-like. The God of Jacob, Who had patiently educated Israel to desire purity more than vice, and holiness more than luxury, had been set aside for an image whose worship was the worship of sin. A nation seeking righteousness is a strong nation. An immoral nation is weak and diseased, falling to ruin and death. This is what Elijah knew.

This is what had brought him to Ahab. The brave and fearless old thinker from the hills stood before the royal throne, and, in the presence of the glittering court, uttered a prophecy.

Elijah's Prophecy in the Court of Proud King Ahab

The prophecy touched nothing of the pomp and might and splendor of the King. It threatened no defeat of his armies, no shadow of death upon his walls. The prophecy concerned such a simple, common thing as rain. But the deep voice of the old man left the King pale and frightened, and struck a sharp terror through the whole court.

"As the Lord God of Israel liveth, before whom I stand," cried Elijah, "there shall not be dew nor rain these years, but according to my word."

That was all he said. That was the message he had come to utter. It was not a little thing for an old and friendless man to confront the proud king of a great nation, and threaten him. But Elijah was heroic of soul. From the midst of the startled and terrified court, the stern old man of God departed and made his lonely way to a brook called Cherith.

Soon the land burned under a blazing sun and cracked into crumbling fissures. Rivers dried up. Even the brook of Cherith was drunk up by the fierce sun. Elijah had taken water from this brook, and ravens had brought him food in the morning and evening. When the brook dried, he departed to a place called Zarephath. The sun scorched him as he went.

As he approached this village, he saw a poor widow gathering a few sticks. She had an only son, and the famine had brought them to beggary. She had a little oil left in a cruse, and a handful of meal in a barrel. She was gathering the sticks to make a last meal for her boy before they both laid down to await death by starvation.

173

Elijah Restores the Son of the
Widow Who Befriends Him

Elijah asked food at her hands in the name of the God of Israel, and promised that the cruse of oil should not fail, nor the barrel of meal waste, till rain came upon the earth. The widow believed, and for a year Elijah lived with her, a year of pitiless sunshine. Then her only son began to sicken, and was brought to the point of death. The widow, in the agony of her grief, laid this calamity at the door of Elijah. The old prophet bade her trust God; he took the child in his arms, and prayed mightily that his life might return. And the Lord heard the voice of Elijah; and the soul of the child came into him again, and he revived.

The widow had trusted in God, but in the hosts of Israel there was nothing but anguish and despair. The faithful said the drought was a punishment. The false said that it was merely an accident of nature. Baal-worship continued. Jezebel, in her palace, watched the skies, and said that soon rain would return.

The Second Meeting
Between King Ahab and Elijah the Thinker

But the cattle were dying like flies, and Ahab, in the face of ruin, sent hither and thither searching for pasture. He himself went with one party, and the chief officer of his household, Obadiah, went at the head of another. They searched every corner of the burning land for green grass, looking at the blazing sky in hope of a cloud. While Obadiah was thus engaged, he came suddenly face to face with the mighty man of God, who bade him go and tell Ahab that Elijah was returned.

The second meeting between the King and the thinker was dramatic. Not humbly came Ahab, but with a darkening brow. "Art thou he that troubleth Israel?" demanded the angry King.

174

"I have not troubled Israel," answered Elijah, "but thou and thy father's house, in that ye have forsaken the commandments of the Lord, and thou hast followed Baal."

The King was silent.

Then Elijah bade Ahab summon to the mountain of Carmel the children of Israel and the prophets of Baal who ate at Jezebel's table, and promised that he would meet them before the world. The hour had come for a trial of strength. The solitary prophet of God was to pit his faith against the priests of Baal and the priests of Astarte, a heathen goddess also worshiped by Jezebel and her people.

This congress stands out in history as a mighty event. On the eastern ridge of the beautiful hill of Carmel, in the clear light of the dawn, were gathered together nearly a thousand false prophets, in their magnificent raiment, and a great host of the debased and brutalized Israelitish people. And there, too, magnificent in his roughness, and solitary in his faith, was Elijah in his robe of camel's hair.

On one side stood a host who served Baal; on the other side a single old man who worshiped the invisible Jehovah. Before them was assembled the nation, with its King.

Elijah stood before the people.

"How long," he cried, "halt ye between two opinions? If the Lord be God, follow Him; but if Baal, then follow him."

At Elijah's challenge two bullocks were slain, one by the priests of Baal, who laid the flesh upon an altar; then at the old man's suggestion the priests were invited to call upon their god to send fire for the altar. The priests of Baal obeyed.

"O Baal, hear us!" The air was filled with their chanting cry. "O Baal, hear us!" Israel looked on and wondered. It seemed a small miracle, a little fire for an altar; Baal would answer by and by. "O Baal, hear us!" The wail of the priests ascended. But no fire came. Elijah marked them till it was noon.

Then the old man lifted up his head and called to the priests:

Here, atop Mount Carmel, the prophet Elijah over-
threw the priests of Baal. A spring gushing forth from
this rock is said to have first appeared on the day that
a water-soaked sacrifice to Jehovah was ignited by
lightning from heaven, thus proving His response to
Elijah's prayer. (I Kings 18:19-40)

"Cry aloud; for he is a god: either he is talking, or he is pursuing, or he is in a journey, or peradventure he sleepeth, and must be awaked."

The priests of Baal cried louder and louder; they cut themselves with knives and lancets; they prostrated themselves. "O Baal, hear us! O Baal, hear us!"

Still there came no answer.

Then Elijah cried in a great voice to the people of Israel: "Come near unto me." He took stones and repaired the broken altar of the true God; and took more stones and built a fresh altar to God. On this altar he laid the flesh of the second bullock. Then he made a trench round the altar, and sent for water and poured it upon the flesh of the bullock, so that all the altar was drenched, and the water ran off and filled the trench. When this was done, in the solemn silence of the sunset hour, Elijah lifted up his voice and prayed:

"Lord God of Abraham, Isaac, and of Israel, let it be known this day that Thou art God in Israel, and that I am Thy servant, and that I have done all these things at Thy word. Hear me, O Lord, hear me, that this people may know that Thou art the Lord God and that Thou hast turned their heart back again."

As this simple prayer died away from the lips of the old man, fire burst from the sticks upon the altar and the air was red with flame.

The Little Cloud That Came Out of the Sea Like a Man's Hand

Israel bowed itself to the dust. A cry arose from all that host: "Jehovah! He is God!" That cry of praise was music in the prophet's ears. God was praised in Israel again!

Then Elijah commanded that the wicked priests of Baal and Astarte should be taken down from the hill and slain. They were a danger to the race. He himself and his servant ascended higher up the mountain. They went up and on till the noise of the multitude was lost to them. Then, in the solitude of the hilltop, Elijah sent his servant to look toward the sea, and he bowed himself in prayer. He was seeking God's blessing for Israel. Six times the servant returned, saying he saw nothing. But the seventh time he brought news. "Behold, there ariseth a little cloud out of the sea, like a man's hand." Then said Elijah, "Go up, say unto Ahab, Prepare thy chariot and get thee down that the rain stop thee not." And Elijah ran before Ahab into the city.

Ahab Makes Haste Home in His Chariot Lest There Should Be Rain

What gracious news for Ahab! To be afraid of rain! To hurry his chariot for fear of rain! Rain for which the land was dying; blessed, life-preserving rain! Black became the heavens; a wind arose, and down through the darkening air descended the floods from the clouds.

But the end was not yet for Elijah. His task was not yet accomplished. And while he waited to finish it, the furious Queen Jezebel sent him word that she would do to him what he had done to her priests of Baal. She threatened him with death on the following day.

Elijah made his way to the wilderness; and when he was spent with the long journey he sank down under a juniper tree, and was very sorrowful.

His work, so it seemed to him, had failed. Jezebel ruled Ahab, and through her Israel was bound in the chains of sin. His battle on Mount Carmel had come to naught. Things remained as they were. He had demonstrated the power of God; but he had not filled Israel with enthusiasm for righteousness.

"It is enough!" cried the old man. "Now, O Lord, take away my life; for I am not better than my fathers."

Elijah cast his mantle over Elisha

Elijah and Elisha

WHILE Elijah lay, broken and dispirited, sleeping under the juniper tree in that waste country near Beersheba, and while it seemed that all his great work had been in vain, an angel appeared to him in his sleep, bidding him go to Mount Horeb.

Elijah obeyed the vision. He made the long journey and took up his quarters in one of the caves of the mountain. As he lodged there, heartbroken and sad, there came to him a voice saying: "What doest thou here, Elijah?"

He knew the voice as the Voice of God. "I have been very jealous for the Lord God of hosts," he made answer; "for the children of Israel have forsaken Thy covenant, thrown down Thine altars, and slain Thy prophets with the sword; and I, even I only, am left."

The Voice commanded him that he should come out from the cave and stand upon the mountain. Elijah obeyed, and while he stood there, a miracle happened.

A great and strong wind rent the mountains, and brake in pieces the rocks before the Lord; but the Lord was not in the wind.

And after the wind, an earthquake. But the Lord was not in the earthquake. And after the earthquake a fire; but the Lord was not in the fire.

Then, when these fierce and terrible things had passed away, and the solemn silence of the great mountain was restored, there came to the ears of the rugged, lonely figure on the rock the sound of a "still small voice."

At that sound the old thinker bowed his head and covered his face with his mantle, for he knew that God was there.

Then the revelation was made to him. Not by great and terrible things does God work among men, but by the still small voice of conscience. There were seven thousand in Israel who had not bowed the knee to Baal. Elijah was to take heart. He was to leave the mountain and go into the ways of men, and work for the triumph of righteousness.

Near to the palace of King Ahab was a little vineyard belonging to a poor man whose name was Naboth. Ahab looked at this vineyard, and it irritated him to think that land so near his palace belonged to another man; he wanted to make it a garden of herbs and possess it for himself. One day he offered to buy the land from Naboth, or to exchange it for a larger and better plot of ground, but Naboth refused the King's offer. The land had belonged to his fathers; to sell or exchange it seemed to him a wicked act. It must descend to his sons.

Ahab was furious at this refusal, and his wicked Queen, Jezebel, wrote in the King's name commanding that Naboth should be stoned to death. All happened as she commanded. Poor Naboth was stoned to death, he and his sons; and the vineyard became the King's property.

Elijah Meets King Ahab and Queen Jezebel in the Vineyard

Then did Ahab rise from his couch, go down from his palace, and step into the vineyard.

He came face to face with Elijah.

Ahab started guiltily and exclaimed: "Hast thou found me, O mine enemy?"

"I have found thee," answered Elijah. "Because thou has sold thyself to do that which is evil in the sight of the Lord, behold, I will bring evil upon thee, and will utterly sweep thee away." And of Jezebel also spoke the Lord, saying, "The dogs shall eat Jezebel by the wall of Jezreel."

Some 3,000 years ago, King Ahab's royal city of Jezreel stood on this site. It is said that his wicked wife, Jezebel, was destroyed here, just as prophesied by Elijah in II Kings 9:30-37.

Ahab was slain in battle, by a man who drew a bow at a venture. The King had feared that he should die, and had gone into the conflict disguised; but the arrow, which was not aimed at him, pierced the joints of his breastplate as he stood in his chariot. He was brought back in this chariot to Samaria, and it was washed of its bloodstains in the very pool beside which Naboth and his sons had been stoned to death.

Elijah was led by God to choose a certain man as his successor. This was Elisha, the son of Shaphat, to whom the old thinker now journeyed. He found Elisha in a field, plowing with twelve yoke of oxen.

Elijah Casts His Mantle Over the Young Man at the Plow

Elijah drew near, looked upon the young man earnestly, and then cast his mantle over him. As he moved away, Elisha ran after him.

He knew he was called to follow this loyal servant of the true God.

The two men, the old thinker and the young prophet, became like father and son, and they testified of God among the people.

At last Elijah was warned that the hour of his death was at hand. He tried to persuade Elisha to leave him, but the young man clung to him.

"As the Lord liveth and as thy soul liveth," he said, "I will not leave thee."

The two passed over Jordan, Elijah striking the waters with his mantle so that they divided and made a path for them. When they came to the other side, Elijah said: "Ask what I shall do for thee, before I be taken away from thee."

And Elisha answered: "I pray thee let a double portion of thy spirit be upon me."

Elijah said: "Thou hast asked a hard thing; nevertheless, if thou see me when I am taken from thee, it shall be so unto thee; but if not, it shall not be so." And as they went on, suddenly there appeared a chariot with horses of fire. And Elisha cried aloud: "My father, my father, the chariot of Israel and the horsemen thereof."

In a moment the chariot separated him from his beloved master. The mantle fell from Elijah's shoulders. The horses sprang forward and upward. Elisha looked, and lo, the great Elijah was passing from the earth; the chariot was moving like a cloud of fire to heaven. Nothing was left of the mighty thinker but his mantle. His work on earth was finished, and his reward had come. Jezebel reigned in her palace; Elijah looked upon God.

Elisha picked up the mantle and stood by the waters of Jordan.

The blessing he had craved from the great prophet came upon him. He received extraordinary power of the spirit. His faith became like a rock.

He soon became famous as a prophet and as a doer of wonderful things; his fame spread into foreign countries. A great man in Syria, Naaman by name, the chief of the whole Syrian army, heard of Elisha's powers from a little Israelite maid who waited upon his wife. Naaman, in the midst of his glory had been stricken with the most hideous affliction; he was a leper.

When he heard of Elisha's power from his wife, Naaman set off with a great retinue, bearing gifts of gold and silver, and appeared before the door of the man of God. Elisha did not come out to him, but sent a message that Naaman should wash in Jordan seven times. This instruction angered the proud soldier.

I thought, he will surely come out to me, and stand and call on the name of the Lord his God, and wave his hand over the place, and recover the leper. Are not Abana and Pharpar, rivers of Damascus, better than all the waters of Israel?

But some of his servants said:

My father, if the prophet had bid thee do some great thing, wouldest thou not have done it? How much rather, then, when he saith to thee, "Wash and be clean."

Naaman accepted the rebuke, and saw the justice of it. He went

Waters from Elisha's Fountain (II Kings 2:19-22) flow through this canal toward modern Jericho, to help keep the "City of Palm Trees" fertile and green.

When Elisha told Naaman the leper to go wash in the River Jordan seven times to be cured of the disease, the Syrian military captain grew angry and replied, "Are not the Abana and Pharpar, rivers of Damascus, better than all the waters of Israel? May I not wash in them and be clean?" (II Kings 5:12) The River Pharpar lies just beyond this dusty Syrian town of Kiswey, near Damascus.

down to the Jordan, dipped seven times, and "his flesh came again like unto the flesh of a little child."

With joy and thanksgiving he offered Elisha precious gifts, but the man of God would take nothing. Then Naaman vowed that he would worship no god but the God of Israel, and asked Elisha to forgive him because, when the King of Syria went to worship his god, Naaman must needs go with him.

And the man of God, touched by this appeal, answered: "Go in peace."

So Naaman departed with joy, astonished by the change that had befallen him, and meditating upon the invisible and eternal God.

As he journeyed, Gehazi, the servant of Elisha, came running secretly, and asked, in his master's name, for gifts for two of the sons of the prophets. Naaman gladly bestowed the gifts, and Gehazi had them in his own house.

Then the wicked servant returned to Elisha, who looked upon him and said: "Whence comest thou, Gehazi?"

The thief answered with a lie. "Thy servant went no whither."

Then said Elisha: "Went not my heart with thee, when the man turned again from his chariot to meet thee? Is it a time to receive money, and to receive garments, and oliveyards, and vineyards, and sheep and oxen, and menservants, and maidservants? The leprosy

Jehu pursued and slew them

of Naaman shall cleave unto thee and unto thy seed for ever."

And Gehazi went out from his presence a leper white as snow.

The Doom of Ahab's House and
Jehu's Ride into the City of Jezreel

Elisha's life was spent in the midst of great political changes and many wars. The love of God grew in Israel, but Jezebel, the queen of the dead Ahab, still worshiped sin and sacrificed to evil in the city of Jezreel.

But now the time was come for the doom foretold by Elijah to fall upon the house of Ahab. Elisha sent a messenger to Jehu, a very valiant man and a bold driver of horses, to anoint him king.

Elisha's messenger came to this great soldier, and, taking him into a secret chamber, anointed him king over Israel, declaring that he should destroy the race of Ahab. Jehu came out, and met with companions who, when they heard what had happened, took off their cloaks, made a throne for their hero, and, blowing on trumpets, shouted: "Jehu is king."

Jehu perceived that he must strike at once. He must reach Jezreel before any warning came to King Joram, who dwelt there with his wicked mother, Jezebel. He sprang into his chariot, calling his followers to drive after him.

Ruins of ancient city of Lachish, captured by King Sennacharib of Assyria from King Hezekiah, son of Ahab. Here, a workman uncovers steps of the king's palace. (II Kings 18:13-37)

A watchman on the tower of Jezreel perceived his coming and a messenger was sent forth to meet the driver of the chariot.

"Thus saith the king, is it peace?"

"What hast thou to do with peace? Turn thee behind me!" cried Jehu.

The watchman on the tower reported what he had seen. A second messenger was sent forth from the city. A like fate befell him. Then said the watchman, seeing the dust about the furious chariot: "The driving is like the driving of Jehu, the son of Nimshi; for he driveth furiously."

"Make ready," said Joram; and horses were harnessed to his chariot.

Then King Joram and King Ahaziah drove out to meet the oncoming Jehu.

Joram called: "Is it peace, Jehu?" and as Jehu made angry answer the wicked kings wheeled about their chariots and fled. But Jehu pursued and slew them.

Thus did the terrible Jehu arrive in the wicked city. And as he entered the streets, Jezebel looked out of the latticed window and cried: "Is it well, thou Zimri, thy master's murderer?"

Jehu looked up quickly.

"Who is on my side? Who?" he cried. Two or three eunuchs looked out. Jehu issued his first command: "Throw her down!"

And that first command was obeyed; the evil woman who had fought against God, who had brought shame to Israel, was hurled from the window by slaves, and Jehu drove his chariot over her.

The Doom of Jezebel and the Last Scenes in the Life of Elisha

Then Jehu entered the palace, and after he had eaten, he said:

"See now to this cursed woman, and bury her; for she is a king's daughter." But his messengers returned quickly from the street. Nothing of Jezebel remained but her skull, her feet and the palms of her hands.

Jehu fulfilled his destiny. He destroyed all the seed of Ahab, and slew the prophets and priests of Baal.

Through all these scenes had lived Elisha; and now, an old man, he felt the hand of God come upon him. The grandson of Jehu was king, and this youth loved Elisha, and wept over him as the shadow of death passed across the aged face of the man of God. He whispered, repeating the famous words: "O my father, my father; the chariots of Israel and the horsemen thereof!"

Then the dying Elisha bade the young King take his bow and shoot, and the string of the bow sang in the room. "The Lord's arrow of victory!" exclaimed Elisha, gazing toward the window.

The man of God closed his eyes, and his spirit passed from the earth.

"Throw her down!"

God and a Man

WHEN Elisha's spirit passed from the earth, another chapter in the strange, eventful history of the Israelites came to an end. The heroic figures had passed away. After some small wars, Israel, as a nation, carried on its business, lived its busy life, and pursued its pleasures with the quiet of an orderly family. Now and again conquests of foreign people fell to its army, and Israel grew strong by its sword, while it waxed rich by its industry; the years passed away without any striking or decisive event of spiritual importance. It was a kingdom neither good nor bad, moving forward to the mystery of the future without concern.

Now, while the Israelites were progressing in this manner, and while apparently there was peace on the earth and security in prosperity, that great shadow which was to fall across their land like an everlasting winter began to show in the heavens. One of the great powers in that day was the kingdom of Assyria. Its strength was amazing, its wealth, prodigious. Everything prospered with it. As an empire it was without a rival in the world, and the capital city of Nineveh was the seat of luxury, pomp, splendor and sin.

It is this period in the history of Nineveh that provides the background for the book of Jonah which is one of the most famous stories in all literature. It has passed into the languages of all nations and the name of its hero is well known in every corner of the globe. There are two great ideas in the story. One is that man can never succeed in running away from God, and the other that God loves all people and will always forgive the sins of those who

Jonah smote them with great terror

epent.

This man Jonah, who was an Israelite and a prophet, received a message from God that he should go to Nineveh and reprove the people for their sins.

But Jonah did not wish to go. The people who lived in Nineveh were enemies of the Jews and Jonah had no desire to save them from their impending doom. He disobeyed God and then tried to flee from God's presence. He thought he would go to a place called Tarshish and wait there till the thought of God's command had left his mind.

So Jonah went to Joppa; and there he found a ship just starting for Tarshish. He paid his fare, got on board, and went down to the innermost part of the ship. Soon after the vessel had got under way, a tempest arose which shook it in all the timbers. The sailors were terrified, and, being superstitious men, they thought that the storm had been sent because some sinner was on board. They cast lots to see whose fault it was, and the lot fell to Jonah. They seized upon the guilty man accordingly, and demanded whence he came and what was his occupation.

Jonah, who was stricken by terror, made answer: "I am an Hebrew; and I fear the Lord, the God of heaven, Which hath made the sea and the dry land."

"What is this thou hast done?" demanded the frightened seamen. "What shall we do unto thee, that the sea may be calm unto us?" For the sea grew more and tempestuous.

And the wretched Jonah cried: "Take me up and cast me into the sea; so shall the sea be calm unto you; for I know that for my sake, this great tempest is come upon you."

The seamen were unwilling to obey; probably they felt sorry for the craven, shrinking figure who cowered from the thought of God's wrath. They rowed hard to get back to land; but it was in vain.

Then they hardened their hearts, and, seizing Jonah, they lifted him up and cast him into the sea.

195

A fisherman mending his nets in much
the same way that his forefathers did in
Bible days.

Now, the story tells us that as Jonah fell through the roaring waters a vast fish loomed through the darkness, opened wide its mouth, and sucked Jonah into it. Uncrushed by the creature's teeth, unbroken by its mighty jaws, the drowning Jonah found himself alive and conscious in the dark depths of its interior. Then Jonah prayed to God, and the fish moved toward the shore, and presently Jonah was vomited forth from the fish and found himself upon dry land.

The Wild Figure of Jonah in the Streets, and a King Sitting in Ashes

Once again God bade the disobedient prophet to go up against Nineveh and this time he obeyed. He made the journey, stood in the streets of the mighty city, and declared that in forty days it should be overthrown.

This declaration terrified the city. Jonah's wild figure created a sensation. His mention of Israel's terrible God threw the Ninevites into a panic. People living in the midst of sin thought suddenly of God and of the end of the world. They were smitten with a great terror.

Instead of singing and dancing, there was a sound of wailing in palaces and mansions. The King himself put on sackcloth, and sat in ashes. A whole city sat in terror, awaiting the end of the world. And their repentance was real. The King said that every man should "cry mightily unto God . . . who knoweth," he said, "whether God will not turn and repent, and turn away from his fierce anger, that we perish not?"

"And God saw their works, that they turned from their evil way; and God repented of the evil that he had said he would do unto them; and he did it not."

So was Nineveh saved, at the warning of Jonah, and the city perished not.

"So Jonah arose and went unto Nineveh
..." (Jonah 3:3)

Isaiah, the Poet and Prophet

AT A time when Israel was much troubled by enemies on every side, there was living in Jerusalem a scholarly and prosperous man named Isaiah, who, far from being a wild and hermit-like man of the mountains, like many of the prophets, was a polished citizen of the great city, a married man, and a father. He is one of the supreme figures in the Old Testament, one of the eternal voices of history. He had lived an easy and aristocratic existence in Jerusalem, enjoying the refinement and culture of the great city, and thinking not very seriously of life or of religion, when a vision came to him. He saw in this vision the glory of heaven and the majesty of God. He heard the song of a great chorus: *Holy, holy, holy, is the Lord of hosts: the whole earth is full of His glory.*

"Woe is me," cried Isaiah, "for I am undone; because I am a man of unclean lips, and I dwell in the midst of a people of unclean lips." Then, in his vision, he saw an angel flying from heaven with a live coal in his hand, and he touched Isaiah's lips with the coal, and said: "Thine iniquity is taken away, and thy sin purged." At this a voice cried from heaven: "Whom shall I send, and who will go for us?" "Here am I," answered Isaiah; "send me." And God sent Isaiah to Israel as a prophet.

The vision altered the whole life of Isaiah. His friends and acquaintances were amazed to find this scholar going about the city as a prophet. His friends were the great people of Jerusalem; he knew kings and the chief priests. And yet he was not afraid to stand up and rebuke the whole nation and prophesy in the name of God.

Isaiah saw, what everybody else saw in that day but with different eyes, how the race of Israel was threatened on every side by

199

The scroll of Isaiah is returned to its place in the ark of the Synagogue. (Scene from the motion picture, "Our Bible— How it Came To Us," produced by the American Bible Society.)

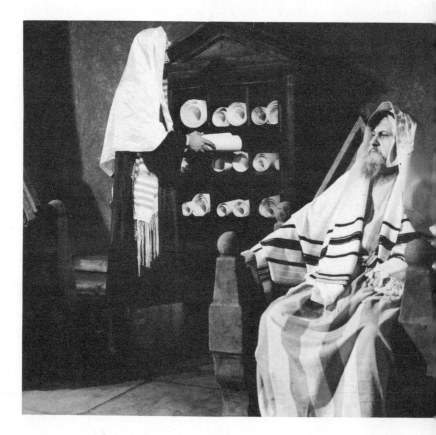

powerful heathen nations. Other people said: "We must get more soldiers," or "We must make friends with our enemies." Isaiah said: "Repent." He saw that it is the character of a nation that matters. He knew that more powerful and dangerous than the enemies of Israel were the sins of Israel.

Now among the enemies of Israel there was none so strong and so threatening as Sennacherib, king of Assyria. As his power waxed greater, and his threat to Israel became more clear, the people in Jerusalem were stricken with terror, and, forsaking their wickedness and heathen idolatries, gave themselves up to worship and prayer and sacrifice. The whole city became a church. But Isaiah was not deceived.

> To what purpose is the multitude of your sacrifices unto Me? saith the Lord; I am full of the burnt offerings of rams and the fat of fed beasts, and I delight not in the blood of bullocks, or of lambs, or of he-goats. . . . Bring no more vain oblations; incense is an abomination unto Me. . . . Your new moons and your appointed feasts My soul hateth; they are a trouble unto Me; I am weary to bear them. . . . When ye make many prayers I will not hear.

Then Isaiah changed his appeal, and thus he called to the people of Israel: "Come now, and let us reason together, saith the Lord; though your sins be as scarlet, they shall be as white as snow; though they be red like crimson they shall be as wool."

Imagine the picture. A whole city shaken by a guilty conscience; smoke and incense suddenly ascending from forsaken altars; temples crowded by prostrated worshipers; priests carefully arranging special feasts and solemn assemblies; fathers and mothers white of face, wondering what will become of their little ones; rich men burying their treasures; politicians whispering that money should be offered to Sennacherib, the enemy at the gates; a long procession of people in the street who talk in low voices together and wait for the hour of doom—a whole city transformed from a place of pride and sin to a whispering place of terror. And in the midst of it the great poet and scholar quietly declaring that God hates

The Valley of Fire, southeast of Jerusalem, where unfaithful kings of Israel once attempted to please God with sacrificial offerings. Of them, God said through Isaiah, "Bring no more vain oblations; incense is an abomination unto me . . ." (Isa. 1:11-13).

these set services and long prayers; that he will have nothing but a clean heart.

Isaiah's Vision of the Power of God, and the Conflict of Good and Evil

The priests thought of God as a great King sitting on a throne and demanding service from men. They thought He would be pleased by incense, sacrifices, long prayers, wailings and beseechings.

Isaiah thought of God as the High and Lofty One Who inhabits Eternity. Before such a God, such an immense Power, how foolish, how mad were the vanity and pride of men! He bade the people turn from the orders of priests and think about the tremendous power of God. God would appear to them, he said, and then how would Israel meet Him?

> In that day a man shall cast away his idols of silver and his idols of gold, which they made for him to worship, to the moles and to the bats; to go into the caverns of the rocks, and into the clefts of the ragged rocks, from before the terror of the Lord, and from the glory of His majesty, when He ariseth to shake mightily the earth.

This was the great conflict of that great hour—the strife between ceremony and truth. The priests cried: "Come to the temple, prostrate yourselves, offer sacrifices, make long prayers." Isaiah, the poet and scholar, said: "Say ye of the righteous, that it shall be well with him. Woe unto the wicked! It shall be ill with him."

It was the great work of Isaiah to make Israel see that God had only one desire for His creatures, their happiness, and therefore their goodness. He made the tremendous revelation, so astonishing to the Israelites and so blasphemous to their priests, that if Israel sinned, God would destroy them, and that if the heathen did good, God would prosper them. God cared neither for sacrifices nor for long prayers, nor for ceremonies; He cared for one thing—*goodness*. God was revealed, not as the special God of Israel, but as the God of righteousness, a Being Who had favored Israel in the past only because of its faith in Him and its devotion to goodness. Isaiah's influence spread. Israel made a great effort to realize God, and to attain righteousness of conduct and sincerity of heart. And God spared them from Sennacherib.

The great army of the Assyrians lay sleeping beside their arms, waiting for the dawn. The sentries watched, leaning on their spears, which were bright in the moonlight. The chariot wheels glistened with dew. The horses were tethered in an immense herd. The stars shone. Tomorrow there would be battle.

Suddenly an angel descended, the Angel of Death; and the proud army of the heathen was stricken, and defeat smote them to dust, without the lifting of a weapon.

Israel was delivered without the casting of a single spear.

The great city was destroyed

The Destruction of a Nation

ISAIAH, the sweetest and most poetic of the prophets, died, and altars were raised in Israel to the heathen gods Baal and Astarte. Human beings were sacrificed to a god called Moloch. The streets of Jerusalem ran with blood, and the whole nation sank into the most horrible depths of superstition and evil. They were as evil as the heathen—more evil, because they had once known righteousness.

God had led them, educated them, shielded them; yet they constantly forgot Him, and deliberately sinned against His Divine Majesty. All about them were heathen nations, rich and powerful. The Israelites, looking at these successful, prosperous neighbors, said to themselves: "Our fathers have declared unto us the stories of Abraham, Isaac and Jacob—but how do we know that they are true? It is all very well for these prophets to tell us of a God we can not see; but how is it that the heathen nations are rich and powerful? *Their* gods do help them; we see it with our eyes. Let us worship Baal and Moloch, and we shall grow strong and rich like the heathen round about us."

But there remained still a remnant in Jerusalem who worshiped the true God, and who waited for His guidance. Through these few, even in the midst of a doomed and wicked city, were to come the salvation and the hope of humanity.

And now the noise of chariot wheels draws near. We see a vast army approaching, the army of Babylon, led by King Nebuchadnezzar. This time no angel of the Lord drives a spear between the oncoming army and the walls of the sacred city. This time Israel is

Destroyed Jewish section of Jerusalem, with the mosque of the Dome of the Rock in the background.

left to depend upon Baal and Moloch. The people whose past was glorious with the names of Moses, Joshua, Saul, David and Solomon, flung themselves down before the images of Baal and Moloch, and waited for their oppressors.

There was now neither pity nor hope. Nebuchadnezzar dashed the last drop of glory from the ancient cup of Israel's greatness, and shattered the cup beneath the wheels of his chariot. All Israel was made captive. This proud people was brought low, to the dust of their enemies, and the great city of Jerusalem gaped to the winds. Israel as a nation was wiped off the face of the earth.

King Nebuchadnezzar conquered Israel

Every Friday on the eve of the Hebrew Sabbath, Jerusalem's pious Jews come to the "Wailing Wall" to read a litany lamenting the destruction of the Temple. Papers bearing prayers are often placed in crevices of the sacred wall, said to be a section of the original Temple built by King Solomon.

Closeup view of the "Wailing Wall" in Jerusalem.

Daniel and the Kings

AMONG the Israelites taken from their native country and carried in captivity to Babylon there were four young men remarkable enough in their talents to be employed by King Nebuchadnezzar in his palace. The chief of these four was Daniel, a youth who saw clearly that all Israel's troubles had been brought about by sinfulness and idolatry. He and his three companions, Shadrach, Meshach and Abed-nego, talked a great deal about these things.

They used to meet in each other's rooms, and discuss what they could do to restore the ancient glory of Israel. They prayed together. They neither ate meat nor drank wine. They kept their bodies in subjection, and devoted all their thoughts to God.

One day there was a stir in the palace. King Nebuchadnezzar had dreamed a dream which had left him with a great awe in his soul; and yet he could not remember the dream, and so he could not tell it to his wise men for their interpretation. Daniel heard of this. He and his friends met and most earnestly prayed that God would reveal to them the forgotten dream and its meaning. This prayer was answered. Daniel stood before the King and revealed to him his dream and its interpretation. So pleased was Nebuchadnezzar that he made Daniel one of his chief men, and advanced Shadrach, Meshach and Abed-nego to places of great honor.

Some time after this the King set up a magnificent image of his god, Bel. He issued a decree that, at a certain hour of a great feast day, everyone should bow down and worship this image. Anyone who refused to obey the command was to be thrown into a burning fiery furnace. Daniel's three friends refused to worship this false god. Certain people, jealous of the Israelites, came and told the King. He was furious. He ordered these Hebrews to be brought before him. They steadily refused, in the King's presence, to obey his order. Nebuchadnezzar asked them angrily if they thought their God could deliver them from a burning fiery furnace, and they replied quietly and calmly that God was able to do so.

Then the King became more angry still, and he commanded that the furnace should be heated seven times hotter. The three friends still refused to worship the idol and thus be false to the one true God. Then they were seized, bound, and hurled by three of the King's strongest captains into the fire. So hot was it that those charged with casting the Israelites into the fire, the three captains, were themselves killed. But lo! in the midst of the great fire, the three walked unharmed, and with them was One Whose form was like the Son of God.

Then the trembling and astonished King called them to come forth from the furnace, and they came out, and not a hair of their heads was singed nor were their clothes scorched.

Nebuchadnezzar, greatly shaken by this extraordinary event, and suddenly changing over to the opposite extreme, ordered that all men should worship the God of Israel, who alone was all-powerful.

But the King himself was soon tired of worshiping an unseen God Who demanded goodness and justice and humility. One night he dreamed another dream which troubled him, and Daniel was sent for, to explain it. Daniel's interpretation was a stern one. The King was to become like the beasts of the field. Daniel implored him to avert this dreadful doom by turning his heart to God. He bade the King "break off his sins by righteousness" and "his iniquities by showing mercy to the poor." For a little while Nebuchadnezzar struggled to obey. But Babylon was a beautiful city. And he who thought his power so great could not humble himself.

"Is not this Babylon great," he cried one day, "which I have built for the honor of my majesty?" At that instant he became mad. The proud and mighty King threw off his royal robes, went out from his palace, and lived with the beasts of the field.

Presently the King's reason returned, and he lived to worship

Daniel was unharmed

the true God, and at last died in the faith of Daniel. But his successor laughed at Israel's God. This king, Belshazzar, made a great feast, and as a jest he sent for the sacred vessels of Jerusalem that his courtiers and his women might drink wine out of them. Suddenly there appeared a man's hand against the wall, writing, and the King and his guests were frozen with fear at sight of strange letters burning on the plaster. The King rose in terror. Wise men were summoned. At last came Daniel, who looked at the words, MENE, MENE, TEKEL, UPHARSIN, and declared aloud: "Mene, God hath numbered thy kingdom, and finished it; Tekel, thou are weighed in the balances and art found wanting; Peres, thy kingdom is divided, and given to the Medes and Persians." (Peres is the plural of Upharsin.)

That night Cyrus, king of the Medes and Persians, captured the city of Babylon, and Belshazzar was slain. Cyrus left Darius the Mede to rule over the city as viceroy, with a council of princes. And in the council was Daniel. The others hated Daniel because of his religion. One day they persuaded Darius to issue a decree that anyone who prayed to gods, instead of only to the King himself, should be flung into a den of lions.

Daniel still prayed. At his open window, which looked toward Jerusalem, he could be seen praying three times every day to the God of Abraham, Isaac and Jacob. His enemies reported this, and Daniel was cast into the den of lions.

The King could not sleep that night, and early in the morning he hurried to the den of lions. He ordered the door, which had been sealed with his own royal seal, to be opened; and there, to his unspeakable relief, he beheld Daniel unharmed among the lions. He embraced the old prophet, implored his forgiveness, and exalted him again to a place of high honor.

Then King Darius wrote unto all people, nations, and languages . . . "I make a decree, that in every dominion of my kingdom men tremble and fear before the God of Daniel: for He is the living God, and steadfast forever—Who hath delivered Daniel from the power of the lions."

How Esther Saved Her People

THE Hebrew people, still captives in a foreign land, were told, some seventy years after the conquest of Jerusalem, that they might return to their sacred city. But, such was the character of this nation, many preferred to remain exiled in Persia, carrying on their trade, and talking of Jerusalem only in a romantic way.

Among the Hebrews who remained in Persia was a man named Mordecai. He had brought up in his home a cousin, a beautiful young girl named Esther. One day soldiers entered the house of Mordecai and bore Esther to the palace of King Ahasuerus. The man who had been a father to Esther must have feared that some terrible thing was about to happen to the maiden; but he was presently amazed to hear that Esther had been chosen by the King as his wife, and that she would henceforth reign as queen over the vast empire of Ahasuerus.

The strange event came about in this manner. A little time before, the King had summoned his queen, Vashti, to show herself at a dishonoring feast, and the brave Queen, not willing to bring shame upon herself, had refused to come. This made the King very angry, and, in a fit of rage, he put the Queen away from him. Then he determined to marry the most beautiful woman in the world, whoever she might be; and his officers were sent far and wide over his great empire to bring before the King all the loveliest young girls in his kingdom. From among these maidens, the King chose little Esther, the cousin of Mordecai, the Hebrew.

Soon after the marriage, Mordecai, who had been advanced to a post of some honor in the King's palace, discovered a plot against the King's life, and for this service his name was entered on the chronicles of the King's house. Now, there was in the court a great prince named Haman, who was jealous of Mordecai; and he

214

thought to get rid of his rival by persuading the King to feel bitterly toward the Hebrew exiles. He told the King that these exiles were dangerous people, that they were upsetting the King's subjects, and he persuaded Ahasuerus to issue a decree that all Hebrews should be destroyed.

Mordecai heard of the plot, and told Esther to intercede with the King on behalf of her people. Esther was loyal to her kindred. But she was a woman, and what Mordecai demanded of her must be done, if done at all, at the risk of her life. For it was a crime punishable by death to approach the King without being summoned to his presence, and for thirty days Esther had not seen her lord. She sent word of this to Mordecai, and Mordecai answered that she herself would surely die if she betrayed her people. Then Esther answered that she would go before the King, and she ended: "If I perish, I perish."

Esther dressed herself in her most beautiful robes, and stood before the King. "When the king saw Esther the queen standing in the court, she obtained favor in his sight . . . then said the king unto her, 'What wilt thou, queen Esther? . . . It shall be given unto thee even unto the half of my kingdom.'"

And she said: "If it seems good unto the king, let the king and Haman come this day unto the banquet that I have prepared for him." The King was much pleased with her request, and granted it. Haman was proud of the honor conferred upon him, but to his wife he said: "Yet all this availeth me nothing, so long as I see Mordecai the Jew sitting at the king's gate."

Then his wife suggested that he should make a high gallows and that in a merry mood he should suggest to the King that Mordecai might be hanged thereon. Now, it chanced that on the very eve of the banquet Ahasuerus, unable to sleep, caused the chronicles of the palace to be read aloud to him; and when he heard of the service of Mordecai, and learned that the man had not been rewarded for saving the King's life, he kept the matter in his heart.

Then entered Haman, in rich robes, and with a happy countenance, intending that he should suggest to the King the hanging of

Mordecai. But before he could speak the King said to him: "What shall be done to the man whom the king delighteth to honor?"

Haman immediately thought that the King referred to him, and answered quickly that such a man, clad in royal robes, crowned with the royal crown, and mounted on the King's own horse, should be led through the streets of the city by one of the King's chief nobles. The idea pleased the King.

"Make haste," he said, "and take the apparel and the horse, as thou hast said, and do even so to Mordecai the Jew, that sitteth at the king's gate: let nothing fail of all that thou hast spoken."

So Haman was humbled to the dust before his enemy; and having conducted Mordecai through the streets, he went home and mourned bitterly.

But at the feast of Queen Esther even worse befell the proud Haman. The young Queen boldly told of Haman's plot against her own life and against all her people; and the King, enraged, ordered that Haman should be hanged on the gallows he had himself prepared for Mordecai.

Then Mordecai was advanced to the highest honors, and thus it came about that the scattered exiles in the mightiest empire of that period had for their ruler a man of their own people who protected them with the scepter of the King. The lot of the exiled Hebrews was made easier from this time. Yet they did not cease to long for the Messiah; they looked forward ever to the coming of the Great Leader.

Esther came before the King

The "King's Dale," outside Jerusalem, showing the entrance to the Tomb of the Prophets, who contributed a number of books to the Holy Bible. Absolom's tomb is at the left, and the Brook Kidron flows at the floor of the valley.

Passageways cut out of rock leading to the tombs of the Judges, on the outskirts of Jerusalem. The Book of Judges tells about those who are buried here.

Selections from
the Greatest of Books

THE Bible is not only a great religious book; it is great literature as well. From it the numberless authors have gained inspiration, and from it they have drawn many of their most striking comparisons. No one can really understand our great poets unless he is familiar with the Bible. For that reason, as well as because it is desirable that the minds of children be filled with lofty thoughts, we have selected here and there a few whole chapters, parts of others, and sometimes single verses, which you will find in the following pages. Every child would be the better for committing them to memory, particularly the Psalms and the sayings of Jesus. They include a very small part of the treasure of the "Book of Books." Following the story given in the pages of this volume, readers will doubtless go to their own copies to read the account of the wanderings and the trials of Israel, and the story of the life of Jesus there given.

A MARVELOUS DESCRIPTION

Remember now thy Creator in the days of thy youth, while the evil days came not, nor the years draw nigh, when thou shalt say, I have no pleasure in them;

While the sun, or the light, or the moon, or the stars, be not darkened, nor the clouds return after the rain:

In the day when the keepers of the house shall tremble, and the strong men shall bow themselves, and the grinders cease because they are few, and those that look out of the windows be darkened.

And the doors shall be shut in the streets, when the sound of the grinding is low, and he shall rise up at the voice of the bird, and all the daughters of music shall be brought low;

Also when they shall be afraid of that which is high, and fears shall be in the way, and the almond tree shall flourish, and the grasshopper shall be a burden, and desire shall fail: because man goeth to his long home, and the mourners go about the streets:

Or ever the silver cord be loosed, or the golden bowl be broken, or the pitcher be broken at the fountain, or the wheel broken at the cistern.

Then shall the dust return to the earth as it was: and the spirit shall return unto God who gave it.

Vanity of vanities, saith the preacher; all is vanity.

And moreover, because the preacher was wise, he still taught the people knowledge; yea, he gave good heed, and sought out, and set in order many proverbs.

The preacher sought to find out acceptable words: and that which was written was upright, even words of truth.

The words of the wise are as goads, and as nails fastened by the masters of assemblies, which are given from one shepherd.

And further, by these, my son, be admonished: of making many books there is no end; and much study is a weariness of the flesh.

Let us hear the conclusion of the whole matter: Fear God, and keep his commandments: for this is the whole duty of man.

For God shall bring every work into judgment, with every secret thing, whether it be good or whether it be evil.

—*Ecclesiastes* 12.

A fisherman of the ancient city of Tyre spreads his
nets to dry in the sun. The prophet Ezekiel prophesied
that boastful Tyre should fall into the sea in the day
of its ruin, and that it would be a place for the spreading of nets. (Ezek. 26:5, 27:27)

Selections From Isaiah

ISAIAH is the best known of the Old Testament prophets. The entire book which bears his name is a message about the greatness and holiness of God who insists that men obey his righteous laws.

Comfort ye, comfort ye my people, saith your God.

Speak ye comfortably to Jerusalem and cry unto her, that her warfare is accomplished, that her iniquity is pardoned; for she hath received of the Lord's hand double for all her sins.

The voice of him that crieth in the wilderness, Prepare ye the way of the Lord, make straight in the desert a highway for our God.

Every valley shall be exalted, and every mountain and hill shall be made low; and the crooked shall be made straight, and the rough places plain.

And the glory of the Lord shall be revealed, and all flesh shall see it together; for the mouth of the Lord hath spoken it.

The voice said, Cry. And he said, What shall I cry? All flesh is grass and all the goodliness thereof is as the flower of the field:

The grass withereth, the flower fadeth; because the spirit of the Lord bloweth upon it; surely the people is grass.

The grass withereth, the flower fadeth; but the word of our God shall stand for ever.

O Zion, that bringest good tidings, get thee up into the high mountain; O Jerusalem, that bringest good tidings, lift up thy voice with strength; lift it up, be not afraid; say unto the cities of Judah, Behold your God!

—Isaiah 40:1–9.

Ho, every one that thirsteth, come ye to the waters, and he that hath no money, come ye, buy, and eat; yea, come, buy wine and milk without money and without price.

Wherefore do ye spend money for that which is not bread? and your labour for that which satisfieth not? hearken diligently unto me, and eat ye that which is good, and let your soul delight itself in fatness.

Incline your ear, and come unto me: hear, and your soul shall live; and I will make an everlasting covenant with you, even the sure mercies of David.

Behold, I have given him for a witness to the people, a leader and commander to the people.

Behold, thou shalt call a nation that thou knowest not, and nations that knew not thee shall run unto thee because of the Lord thy God, and for the Holy One of Israel; for he hath glorified thee.

Seek ye the Lord while he may be found, call ye upon him while he is near:

Let the wicked forsake his way, and the unrighteous man his thoughts: and let him return unto the Lord, and he will have mercy upon him; and to our God, for he will abundantly pardon.

For my thoughts are not your thoughts, neither are your ways my ways, saith the Lord.

For as the heavens are higher than the earth, so are my ways higher than your ways, and my thoughts than your thoughts.

For as the rain cometh down, and the snow from heaven, and returneth not thither, but watereth the earth, and maketh it bring forth and bud, that it may give seed to the sower, and bread to the eater:

So shall my word be that goeth forth out of my mouth: it shall not return unto me void, but it shall accomplish that which I please, and it shall prosper in the things whereto I sent it.

For ye shall go out with joy, and be led forth with peace: the mountains and the hills shall break forth before you into singing, and all the trees of the field shall clap their hands.

Instead of the thorn shall come up the fir tree, and instead of the brier shall come up the myrtle tree: and it shall be to the Lord for a name, for an everlasting sign that shall not be cut off.

—Isaiah 55.

"Sow to yourselves in righteousness, reap in mercy."
(Hosea 10:12)

The Book of Proverbs

ONE of the most interesting sections of the whole Bible is the Book of Proverbs, which the old writers said were the sayings of Solomon, the wise King of Israel. It contains much praise of wisdom and advice to avoid folly. There are hundreds of short verses, most of them only two lines long, showing usually contrasting good and evil, wisdom and folly, or success and failure. Though our times differ in many ways from the times when the proverbs were first written, they show such insight into human nature that they are as valuable now as then. Here follow a few extracts.

Boast not thyself of to-morrow;
For thou knowest not what a day may bring forth.
Let another man praise thee, and not thine own mouth;
A stranger, and not thine own lips.
A stone is heavy, and the sand weighty;
But a fool's wrath is heavier than them both.
Wrath is cruel, and anger is outrageous;
But who is able to stand before envy?
Open rebuke is better than secret love.
Faithful are the wounds of a friend;
But the kisses of an enemy are deceitful

. . . .

A soft answer turneth away wrath:
But grievous words stir up anger.
The tongue of the wise useth knowledge aright:
But the mouth of fools poureth out foolishness.
The eyes of the Lord are in every place,
Beholding the evil and the good.
A wholesome tongue is a tree of life:

But perverseness therein is a breach in the spirit.
A fool despiseth his father's instruction:
But he that regardeth reproof is prudent.

. . . . .

A good name is rather to be chosen than great riches,
And loving favour rather than silver and gold.
The rich and poor meet together:
The Lord is the maker of them all.
A prudent man foreseeth the evil, and hideth himself:
But the simple pass on, and are punished.
By humility and the fear of the Lord
Are riches, and honour, and life.
Thorns and snares are in the way of the froward:
He that doth keep his soul shall be far from them.
Train up a child in the way he should go:
And when he is old, he will not depart from it.

. . . . . .

If riches be a possession to be desired in this life, what is richer
than wisdom, that worketh all things?

And if prudence work, who of all that are is a more cunning
workman than she?

A VIRTUOUS WOMAN

In ancient times each household manufactured a large part of what
was necessary for comfort. Here is a wonderful description of the
work of the house mother in those early times, before factories had
developed. The woman of the house had much the same duties in
the early days of our own country.

Who can find a virtuous woman?
For her price is far above rubies.
The heart of her husband doth safely trust in her.
So that he shall have no need of spoil.
She will do him good and not evil
All the days of her life.
She seeketh wool, and flax,
And worketh willingly with her hands.

She is like the merchants' ships;
She bringeth her food from afar.
She riseth also while it is yet night,
And giveth meat to her household,
And a portion to her maidens.
She considereth a field, and buyeth it:
With the fruit of her hands she planteth a vineyard.
She girdeth her loins with strength,
And strengtheneth her arms.
She perceiveth that her merchandise is good:
Her candle goeth not out by night.
She layeth her hands to the spindle,
And her hands hold the distaff.
She stretcheth out her hand to the poor;
Yea, she reacheth forth her hands to the needy.
She is not afraid of the snow for her household:
For all her household are clothed with scarlet.
She maketh herself coverings of tapestry;
Her clothing is silk and purple.
Her husband is known in the gates,
When he sitteth among the elders of the land
She maketh fine linen, and selleth it;

229

The market place in the Old City of Jerusalem, alive with life, noise and news.

And delivereth girdles unto the merchant.
Strength and honour are her clothing;
And she shall rejoice in time to come.
She openeth her mouth with wisdom;
And her tongue is the law of kindness.
She looketh well to the ways of her household,
And eateth not the bread of idleness.
Her children arise up, and call her blessed.

From the Psalms of David

THE master-note of the Psalms is Happiness. To obtain happiness we must think. Praise of God is not given by merely singing and praying, but chiefly by *thought*. We should think about God, and get into the habit of thinking constantly about His power, His eternity, His delight in beautiful things, His kindness and His love. Sit quite still, and with closed eyes think that this wonderful world, with its rolling waters, its high mountains, its green pastures, and its pageant of scented flowers, is the work of One Who existed before the earth was made, and will exist when you are laid in the grave. David was the great *thinker*. He thought about God, and God became real to him. If you do not think of God often and quietly and for a long space at a time you will never know the chief happiness of existence, which is the certainty that the great Creator cares for you and has prepared for you everlasting pleasures. David's message to the world is: *Think about God*. We give here a selection from his Psalms.

PSALM 1

In this song David teaches the great lesson that only those people who think of God in all things can be happy; and that sooner or later people who live as if there were no God will find out their dreadful mistake. The good man is wise; the godless man is foolish.

Blessed is the man that walketh not in the counsel of the ungodly, nor standeth in the way of sinners, nor sitteth in the seat of the scornful.

2. But his delight is in the law of the Lord; and in his law doth he meditate day and night.

3. And he shall be like a tree planted by the rivers of water, that bringeth forth his fruit in his season; his leaf also shall not wither; and whatsoever he doeth shall prosper.

4. The ungodly are not so: but are like the chaff which the wind driveth away.

5. Therefore the ungodly shall not stand in the judgment, nor sinners in the congregation of the righteous.

6. For the Lord knoweth the way of the righteous: but the way of the ungodly shall perish.

PSALM 23

This is the perfect song of faith. We are all like sheep, and watching over us is a Shepherd, Who knows our wants and will protect our weakness from the wolves. David had thought so much of God's kindness and the beauty of God's world, that he felt certain God was leading him to even greater joy and peace. "I shall not want." Every man who loves the earth, and feels the beauty of God's work, knows that he will never want.

The Lord is my shepherd; I shall not want.

2. He maketh me to lie down in green pastures: he leadeth me beside the still waters.

3. He restoreth my soul: he leadeth me in the paths of righteousness for his name's sake.

4. Yea, though I walk through the valley of the shadow of death, I will fear no evil: for thou art with me; thy rod and thy staff they comfort me.

5. Thou preparest a table before me in the presence of mine enemies: thou anointest my head with oil; my cup runneth over.

6. Surely goodness and mercy shall follow me all the days of my

233

"The Lord is my shepherd; I shall not want." (Ps. 23:1) A Palestine shepherd, with the Mount of the Beatitudes in the background.

Sifting wheat in the Holy Land. Forksful of grain are thrown into the air, and the wind carries away the light chaff with the heavy grain falling to the floor. This is one of many primitive methods of agriculture still in use in the Holy Land.

"Yea, though I walk through the valley of the shadow of death,
I will fear no evil: for thou art with me . . ." (Ps. 23:4)

life: and I will dwell in the house of the Lord for ever.

PSALM 24

David was a lover of nature. He knew the green earth like a book. He learned the great lesson, that those who are not vain and frivolous and taken up with riches and business can feel God's presence in the freshness of the dawn and the solemn majesty of the sunset.

The earth is the Lord's, and the fulness thereof; the world, and they that dwell therein.

2. For he hath founded it upon the seas, and established it upon the floods.

3. Who shall ascend into the hill of the Lord? or who shall stand in his holy place?

4. He that hath clean hands, and a pure heart; who hath not lifted up his soul unto vanity, nor sworn deceitfully.

5. He shall receive the blessing from the Lord, and righteousness from the God of his salvation.

6. This is the generation of them that seek him, that seek thy face, O Jacob.

7. Lift up your heads, O ye gates; and be ye lifted up, ye everlasting doors; and the King of glory shall come in.

8. Who is this King of glory? The Lord strong and mighty, the Lord mighty in battle.

9. Lift up your heads, O ye gates; even lift them up, ye everlasting doors; and the King of glory shall come in.

10. Who is this King of glory? The Lord of hosts, he is the King of glory.

PSALM 27

Here again is a noble utterance from a soul safe under God's overshadowing wings. David felt the nearness of God because he felt the beauty of the earth and the power of the universe. He was sure of God. In that faith he felt that nothing could hurt him. His last word is "wait." If not in this world, then in the next, God will make all things plain.

The Lord is my light and my salvation; whom shall I fear? The Lord is the strength of my life; of whom shall I be afraid?

2. When the wicked, even mine enemies and my foes, came upon me to eat up my flesh, they stumbled and fell.

3. Though an host should encamp against me, my heart shall not fear: though war should rise against me, in this will I be confident.

4. One thing have I desired of the Lord, that will I seek after; that I may dwell in the house of the Lord all the days of my life, to behold the beauty of the Lord, and to inquire in his temple.

5. For in the time of trouble he shall hide me in his pavilion: in the secret of his tabernacle shall he hide me; he shall set me up upon a rock.

6. And now shall mine head be lifted up above mine enemies round about me: therefore will I offer in his tabernacle sacrifices of joy; I will sing, yea, I will sing praises unto the Lord.

7. Hear, O Lord, when I cry with my voice: have mercy also upon me, and answer me.

8. When thou saidst, Seek ye my face; my heart said unto thee, Thy face, Lord, will I seek.

9. Hide not thy face far from me; put not thy servant away in anger: thou hast been my help; leave me not, neither forsake me, O God of my salvation.

10. When my father and my mother forsake me, then the Lord will take me up.

11. Teach me thy way, O Lord, and lead me in a plain path, be-

cause of mine enemies.

12. Deliver me not over unto the will of mine enemies: for false witnesses are risen up against me, and such as breathe out cruelty.

13. I had fainted, unless I had believed to see the goodness of the Lord in the land of the living.

14. Wait on the Lord: be of good courage, and he shall strengthen thine heart: wait, I say, on the Lord.

PSALM 34

Here is noble music: "O taste and see that the Lord is gracious." People do not think about God, or they would know that there is no happiness like that which comes from realizing the eternity and the power of the great, kind, gentle God. He is a fool who does not fear God. How can mortal man, who *must* die, do anything but feel reverence for a Being who is eternal and almighty? To fear God is to trust Him; to trust Him is to be unafraid of death.

I will bless the Lord at all times: his praise shall continually be in my mouth.

2. My soul shall make her boast in the Lord: the humble shall hear thereof, and be glad.

3. O magnify the Lord with me, and let us exalt his name together.

4. I sought the Lord, and he heard me, and delivered me from all my fears.

5. They looked unto him, and were lightened: and their faces were not ashamed.

6. This poor man cried, and the Lord heard him, and saved him out of all his troubles.

7. The angel of the Lord encampeth round about them that fear him, and delivereth them.

8. O taste and see that the Lord is good: blessed is the man that trusteth in him.

9. O fear the Lord, ye his saints: for there is no want to them that fear him.

10. The young lions do lack, and suffer hunger: but they that seek the Lord shall not want any good thing.

11. Come, ye children, hearken unto me: I will teach you the fear of the Lord.

12. What man is he that desireth life, and loveth many days, that he may see good?

13. Keep thy tongue from evil, and thy lips from speaking guile.

14. Depart from evil, and do good; seek peace, and pursue it.

15. The eyes of the Lord are upon the righteous, and his ears are open unto their cry.

16. The face of the Lord is against them that do evil, to cut off the remembrance of them from the earth.

17. The righteous cry, and the Lord heareth and delivereth them out of all their troubles.

18. The Lord is nigh unto them that are of a broken heart; and saveth such as be of a contrite spirit.

19. Many are the afflictions of the righteous: but the Lord delivereth him out of them all.

20. He keepeth all his bones: not one of them is broken.

21. Evil shall slay the wicked: and they that hate the righteous shall be desolate

22. The Lord redeemeth the soul of his servants: and none of them that trust in him shall be desolate.

PSALM 46

This is one of the greatest songs of triumph. The man who believes in God is unconquerable by the world. No one can hurt him: no sorrow can bow him down. In the midst of disaster, he closes his eyes, folds his hands, and is *still*—holding the thought of God's power and love, and knowing that he is safe. "Be still, and know that I am God." Noisy people never know the joy of drawing near to God by thought.

God is our refuge and strength, a very present help in trouble.

2. Therefore will not we fear, though the earth be removed, and though the mountains be carried into the midst of the sea.

3. Though the waters thereof roar and be troubled, though the

mountains shake with the swelling thereof.

4. There is a river, the streams whereof shall make glad the city of God, the holy place of the tabernacle of the most High.

5. God is in the midst of her; she shall not be moved: God shall help her, and that right early.

6. The heathen raged, the kingdoms were moved: he uttered his voice, the earth melted.

7. The Lord of hosts is with us; the God of Jacob is our refuge.

8. Come, behold the works of the Lord, what desolations he hath made in the earth.

9. He maketh wars to cease unto the end of the earth; he breaketh the bow, and cutteth the spear in sunder; he burneth the chariot in the fire.

10. Be still, and know that I am God; I will be exalted among the heathen, I will be exalted in the earth.

11. The Lord of hosts is with us: the God of Jacob is our refuge.

PSALM 90

This mighty Psalm brings home to every sensible and thoughtful person the shortness of man's life, and the eternity and power of High God. Generations pass away like waves moving to the shore. God remaineth. If anyone will but "number his days"—that is to say, if he will *think* how every day of his life he is but hurrying toward the mystery of death, surely he will bow himself before a Power which exists for ever and ever and is omnipotent. Compare the grandest buildings in the world with a single weed in the garden. Then think of the pageant of the stars, the march of the worlds in space. Let the beauty of God be upon you.

Lord, thou has been our dwelling-place in all generations.

2. Before the mountains were brought forth, or ever thou hadst formed the earth and the world, even from everlasting to everlasting, thou art God.

3. Thou turnest man to destruction; and sayest, Return, ye children of men.

4. For a thousand years in thy sight are but as yesterday when it is past, and as a watch in the night.

241

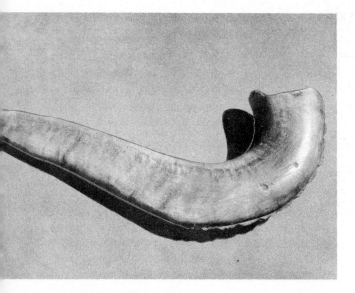

The Shofar, or ram's horn, for countless generations has been sounded on Rosh Hashana —the Jewish New Year—signifying the time of man's annual inscription in the Book of Life. This traditional curved trumpet is mentioned in Psalm 81:3.

"Thy presses shall burst out with new wine." (Prov. 3:10) An old olive hand-press in Trans-Jordan.

5. Thou carriest them away as with a flood; they are as a sleep; in the morning they are like grass which groweth up.

6. In the morning it flourisheth, and groweth up; in the evening it is cut down, and withereth.

7. For we are consumed by thine anger, and by thy wrath are we troubled.

8. Thou hast set our iniquities before thee, our secret sins in the light of thy countenance.

9. For all our days are passed away in thy wrath; we spend our years as a tale that is told.

10. The days of our years are threescore years and ten; and if by reason of strength they be fourscore years, yet is their strength labour and sorrow; for it is soon cut off, and we fly away.

11. Who knoweth the power of thine anger? even according to thy fear, so is thy wrath.

12. So teach us to number our days, that we may apply our hearts unto wisdom.

13. Return, O Lord, how long? and let it repent thee concerning thy servants.

14. O satisfy us early with thy mercy; that we may rejoice and be glad all our days.

15. Make us glad according to the days wherein thou hast afflicted us, and the years wherein we have seen evil.

16. Let thy work appear unto thy servants, and thy glory unto their children.

17. And let the beauty of the Lord our God be upon us; and establish thou the work of our hands upon us; yea, the work of our hands establish thou it.

PSALM 15

This psalm, attributed to David, tells us that a good man will not spread slanders against his neighbors.

> Lord, who shall abide in thy tabernacle?
> Who shall dwell in thy holy hill?
> He that walketh uprightly, and worketh righteousness,
> And speaketh the truth in his heart.
> He that backbiteth not with his tongue,

"The heavens declare the glory of God;
And the firmament showeth His handi-
work." (Ps. 19:1)

"O send out Thy light and Thy truth; let them lead me."
(Ps. 43:3)

"Thou crownest the year with Thy goodness..."
(Ps. 65:11)

"O Lord, how manifold are Thy works!"
(Ps. 104:24)

Nor doeth evil to his neighbour,
Nor taketh up a reproach against his neighbour.
In whose eyes a vile person is contemned;
But he honoureth them that fear the Lord.
He that sweareth to his own hurt, and changeth not.
He that putteth not out his money to usury,
Nor taketh reward against the innocent.
He that doeth these things shall never be moved.

PSALM 103

Here David is in his happiest mood. He is full of thankfulness. The thought of God's greatness and kindness has taken hold of him. He feels how small is man: how infinite and wonderful is the Creator. Man is safe because God is so great. The thought of the mercy of God—that is, His kindness, made David so happy that he sang in his joy.

Bless the Lord, O my soul: and all that is within me, bless his holy name.

2. Bless the Lord, O my soul, and forget not all his benefits:

3. Who forgiveth all thine iniquities; who healeth all thy diseases;

4. Who redeemeth thy life from destruction; who crowneth thee with loving-kindness and tender mercies;

5. Who satisfieth thy mouth with good things; so that thy youth is renewed like the eagle's.

6. The Lord executeth righteousness and judgment for all that are oppressed.

7. He made known his ways unto Moses, his acts unto the children of Israel.

8. The Lord is merciful and gracious, slow to anger, and plenteous in mercy.

9. He will not always chide; neither will he keep his anger for ever.

10. He hath not dealt with us after our sins, nor rewarded us according to our iniquities.

"Bless the Lord . . . Who satisfieth thy
mouth with good things . . ." (Ps. 103:5)
A grape seller on a street corner in
Jerusalem.

11. For as the heaven is high above the earth, so great is his mercy toward them that fear him.

12. As far as the east is from the west, so far hath he removed our transgressions from us.

13. Like as a father pitieth his children, so the Lord pitieth them that fear him.

14. For he knoweth our frame; he remembereth that we are dust.

15. As for man, his days are as grass: as a flower of the field, so he flourisheth.

16. For the wind passeth over it, and it is gone; and the place thereof shall know it no more.

17. But the mercy of the Lord is from everlasting to everlasting upon them that fear him, and his righteousness unto children's children;

18. To such as keep his covenant, and to those that remember his commandments to do them.

19. The Lord hath prepared his throne in the heavens; and his kingdom ruleth over all.

20. Bless the Lord, ye his angels, that excel in strength, that do his commandments, hearkening unto the voice of his word.

21. Bless ye the Lord, all ye his hosts; ye ministers of his, that do his pleasure.

22. Bless the Lord, all his works in all places of his dominion: bless the Lord, O my soul.

PSALM 137

In this Psalm Israel is reminded of its unhappiness. Sorrow and suffering are certain to follow forgetfulness of God. When we forget God and fall into sin, we are taken captive by our own foolishness. It is hard then to sing the happy songs of joy in God's Fatherhood. We are prisoners. We are not free.

By the rivers of Babylon, there we sat down; yea, we wept, when we remembered Zion.

2. We hanged our harps upon the willows in the midst thereof.

3. For there they that carried us away captive required of us a song; and they that wasted us required of us mirth, saying, Sing us

one of the songs of Zion.

4. How shall we sing the Lord's song in a strange land?

5. If I forget thee, O Jerusalem, let my right hand forget her cunning.

6. If I do not remember thee, let my tongue cleave to the roof of my mouth; if I prefer not Jerusalem above my chief joy.

7. Remember, O Lord, the children of Edom in the day of Jerusalem; who said, Rase it, rase it, even to the foundation thereof.

8. O daughter of Babylon, who art to be destroyed; happy shall he be, that rewardeth thee as thou hast served us.

9. Happy shall he be, that taketh and dasheth thy little ones against the stones.

PSALM 19

This magnificent song, which begins by finding God in nature—a favorite with all who love the sublime—turns into a song of praise and appreciation and ends by asking humbly for help against temptations which are everywhere about us.

The heavens declare the glory of God;
And the firmament sheweth his handywork.
Day unto day uttereth speech,
And night unto night sheweth knowledge.
There is no speech nor language,
Where their voice is not heard.
Their line is gone out through all the earth,
And their words to the end of the world.
In them hath he set a tabernacle for the sun,
Which is as a bridegroom coming out of his chamber,
And rejoiceth as a strong man to run a race.
His going forth is from the end of the heaven,
And his circuit unto the ends of it:
And there is nothing hid from the heat thereof.
The law of the Lord is perfect, converting the soul:
The testimony of the Lord is sure, making wise the simple.
The statutes of the Lord are right, rejoicing the heart:
The commandment of the Lord is pure, enlightening the eyes.

The fear of the Lord is clean, enduring for ever:
The judgments of the Lord are true and righteous altogether.
More to be desired are they than gold, yea, than much fine gold:
Sweeter also than honey and the honeycomb.
Moreover by them is thy servant warned:

And in keeping of them there is great reward.
Who can understand his errors?
Cleanse thou me from secret faults.
Keep back thy servant also from presumptuous sins;
Let them not have dominion over me:
Then shall I be upright,
And I shall be innocent from the great transgression.
Let the words of my mouth,
And the meditation of my heart, be acceptable in thy sight,
O Lord, my strength, and my redeemer.

PSALM 42

Troubles came upon Israel and it seemed sometimes that God was
no longer watching over them, for the heathen oppressed the
people. Yet here the sons of Korah declare that God has not forgotten his people.

As the hart panteth after the water brooks,
So panteth my soul after thee, O God.
My soul thirsteth for God, for the living God:
When shall I come and appear before God?
My tears have been my meat day and night,
While they continually say unto me, Where is thy God?
When I remember these things, I pour out my soul in me:
For I had gone with the multitude, I went with them to the house
  of God,
With the voice of joy and praise, with a multitude that kept holy-
  day.
Why art thou cast down, O my soul? and why art thou disquieted
  in me?
Hope thou in God: for I shall yet praise him

For the help of his countenance.

O my God, my soul is cast down within me: therefore will I remember thee

From the land of Jordan, and of the Hermonites, from the hill Mizar.

Deep calleth unto deep at the noise of thy waterspouts:

All thy waves and thy billows are gone over me.

Yet the Lord will command his lovingkindness in the daytime,

And in the night his song shall be with me,

And my prayer unto the God of my life.

I will say unto God my rock, Why hast thou forgotten me?

Why go I mourning because of the oppression of the enemy?

As with a sword in my bones, mine enemies reproach me;

While they say daily unto me, Where is thy God?

Why art thou cast down, O my soul? and why art thou disquieted within me?

Hope thou in God: for I shall yet praise him,

Who is the health of my countenance, and my God.

PSALM 84

This psalm which we are told was written by one of the sons of Korah has not the same joyousness as some of those attributed to David. Yet it shows great faith, and some of the verses are known to all.

How amiable are thy tabernacles, O Lord of hosts!

My soul longeth, yea, even fainteth for the courts of the Lord:

My heart and my flesh crieth out for the living God.

Yea, the sparrow hath found an house,

And the swallow a nest for herself, where she may lay her young,

Even thine altars, O Lord of hosts, my King, and my God.

Blessed are they that dwell in thy house:

They will be still praising thee.

Blessed is the man whose strength is in thee:

In whose heart are the ways of them.

Who passing through the valley of Baca make it a well;

The rain also filleth the pools.

They go from strength to strength,

Every one of them in Zion appeareth before God.
O Lord God of hosts, hear my prayer:
Give ear, O God of Jacob.
Behold, O God our shield,
And look upon the face of thine anointed.
For a day in thy courts is better than a thousand.
I had rather be a doorkeeper in the house of my God,
Than to dwell in the tents of wickedness.
For the Lord God is a sun and shield:
The Lord will give grace and glory:
No good thing will he withhold from them that walk uprightly.
O Lord of Hosts,
  Blessed is the man that trusteth in thee.

PSALM 91

Here we have a song of faith. The writer declares that God will take care of those who put their trust in Him, and will bring them safely through the dangers and perils seen and unseen.

He that dwelleth in the secret place of the Most High
Shall abide under the shadow of the Almighty.
I will say of the Lord, He is my refuge and my fortress:

  My God; in him will I trust.
  Surely he shall deliver thee from the snare of the fowler,
  And from the noisome pestilence.
  He shall cover thee with his feathers,
  And under his wings shalt thou trust:
  His truth shall be thy shield and buckler.
  Thou shalt not be afraid for the terror by night;
  Nor for the arrow that flieth by day;
  Nor for the pestilence that walketh in darkness;
  Nor for the destruction that wasteth at noonday.
  A thousand shall fall at thy side,
  And ten thousand at thy right hand;
  But it shall not come nigh thee.
  Only with thine eyes shalt thou behold

And see the reward of the wicked.
Because thou hast made the Lord, which is my refuge,
Even the Most High, thy habitation;
There shall no evil befall thee,
Neither shall any plague come nigh thy dwelling.
For he shall give his angels charge over thee,
To keep thee in all thy ways.
They shall bear thee up in their hands,
Lest thou dash thy foot against a stone.
Thou shalt tread upon the lion and adder:
The young lion and the dragon shalt thou trample under feet.
Because he hath set his love upon me, therefore will I deliver him:
I will set him on high, because he hath known my name.
He shall call upon me, and I will answer him.
I will be with him in trouble;
I will deliver him, and honour him.
With long life will I satisfy him,
And shew him my salvation.

Praise the Lord with harp: sing unto him with the psaltery and an
    instrument of ten strings.
Sing unto him a new song; play skilfully with a loud noise.
For the word of the Lord is right; and all his works are done in
    truth.
He loveth righteousness and judgment: the earth is full of the good-
    ness of the Lord.